Presented To:

_____

From:

_____

Date:

_____

School of the
supernatural

School of the supernatural

LIVE THE
SUPERNATURAL
LIFE THAT GOD
CREATED YOU
TO LIVE

RYAN WYATT

DESTINY IMAGE® PUBLISHERS, INC.

P.O. Box 310, Shippensburg, PA 17257-0310

"Speaking to the Purposes of God for This Generation and for the Generations to Come."

This book and all other Destiny Image, Revival Press, MercyPlace, Fresh Bread, Destiny Image Fiction, and Treasure House books are available at Christian bookstores and distributors worldwide.

For a U.S. bookstore nearest you, call 1-800-722-6774.

For more information on foreign distributors, call 717-532-3040.

Reach us on the Internet: www.destinyimage.com.

ISBN 13 TP: 978-0-7684-3791-1

ISBN 13 HC: 978-0-7684-3792-8

ISBN 13 LP: 978-0-7684-3793-5

ISBN 13 E-book: 978-0-7684-8992-7

For Worldwide Distribution, Printed in the U.S.A.

3 4 5 6 7 8 9 10 11 / 13 12 11

Dedication

I dedicate this book to my younger brother, Kenneth (Kenny) Wyatt. He was killed in a car accident on his 26th birthday, the week of Christmas. He knew Jesus, and today he is in heaven. His was the first funeral I ever performed. In celebrating Christmas, the moment that our Heavenly Father gave His greatest offering into the earth, His own Son...I and my family gave and sowed our greatest offering into the heavens, my brother. He died at the intersection of Joshua Road and Love's Chapel Road. I chose the day of his funeral, to sow him as a seed, believing for a great Joshua army of believers to be raised up that will conquer their Promised Land and wage a war of love! I continue to fight for this on the earthly side and Kenneth continues to fight for this on the eternal side. Together, we are partners in ministry.

I know that this book is the first of many that I will write... But Kenneth, I dedicate this book to you as a first-fruits of many books that I know will impact entire generations of believers that will fall in love with Jesus and impact this world for the Kingdom of God. Until that time in my future when we are reunited in eternity's realm...I say, *I give all for God and His Kingdom*!

Acknowledgments

Kelly Wyatt, my amazing wife and ministry partner! You are one of God's greatest gifts to me and our boys. You make living life such an amazing experience and I'm forever grateful for you!

Steve and Melinda Wyatt, my parents. Your support throughout my life has served as a foundation for my ministry today. "Thank You" can't possibly describe how grateful I am for your love and support.

Abiding Glory Leadership and Church Family...You all are amazing and I treasure each of you as family. It is an honor to advance the Kingdom with you!

Endorsements

With biblical clarity and fresh faith for today, Ryan Wyatt brings us a treasure chest of revelation on how you can rise above the natural into a supernatural lifestyle. Join him and a new generation of believers who believe that the nature and power of Jesus follow true disciples in our time.

JAMES W GOLL
Encounters Network
Author of *The Seer, The Lost Art of Intercession, Deliverance from Darkness,* and many more

The first time I heard Ryan speak I knew he was very gifted in the Spirit and taught with supernatural wisdom. This book should be mandatory discipleship for all that want to walk in the fullness of all the gifts of the Spirit.

SID ROTH
Host, *It's Supernatural*

The prophet Joel prophesied an end of the age army that would be a "great and mighty people" whose appearance is like "the appearance of horses; and like war horses, so they run." Undeniably, we are living in the days when this great prophecy will become a living reality. Throughout the Body of Christ various voices are heralding this message; Ryan Wyatt is one such voice. With biblical precision and prophetic accuracy Ryan, in his book, *School of the Supernatural* highlights sound truth to identify and equip this forthcoming army. The attributes of humility, integrity, and power will be woven into the identities of this group. The book that you hold in your hands will help facilitate these divine virtues and point people to intimacy and fellowship with the Lord Jesus. All of this will be for the purpose of the harvest and to see the Lord receive the full measure of His reward.

PAUL KEITH DAVIS
WhiteDove Ministries, Founder

Ryan Wyatt is deeply profound, scripturally solid, and gloriously practical in his teachings on the supernatural realms of the Kingdom of God. I have often sat under his ministry and hung on every word. *School of the Supernatural* is not only a book that will deeply influence your faith, it is one that every believer should have in his or her resource library.

PATRICIA KING
Founder XPmedia
Xpmedia.com

School of the Supernatural with Ryan Wyatt proclaims that it is the Christian's right to live a supernatural lifestyle filled with God's presence and power. I believe this book will be a great blessing to you as you learn how to operate in the power of the Kingdom and live in the realm of true authentic Christianity.

MATT SORGER
Host of TV's *Power for Life*
Matt Sorger Ministries

From its early beginnings I have seen the development of Ryan's *School of the Supernatural*. I have seen the development of the material to the point where it is now an excellent tool in the hands of anyone who is hungry for the works of God to be evident in his or her life. This new edition comes fully recommended and fully proven for this up and coming generation of "God workers"

DEREK BROWN
KC21

Ryan Wyatt's book *School of the Supernatural* will stir you to dive deeper into the things of the Lord. With great pleasure, I highly recommend this book by Ryan Wyatt, I've known Ryan for many years, he has a wonderful anointing. His book will help release those who are hungry into a deeper place in God and help them to see the impossible become possible in day-to-day living. Get ready to receive fresh revelation that releases fresh anointing from the Lord as you dive into this book.

BOBBY CONNER
Founder Eagles View Ministries
www.bobbyconner.org

In the midst of a great outpouring of God's grace, love, and power many of us have been left longing for still *more* of Him. In his book *School of the Supernatural*

Ryan Wyatt takes us deep into the Secret Place where we can experience God's Presence on earth as it is in Heaven.

JOHN ARNOTT
Founding Pastor of Catch the Fire Ministries
(formally Toronto Airport Christian Fellowship)

This book gives an excellent teaching on how to learn the difference between the soul, which, is the mind, will, and emotion and the spiritual realm, which is your conscience (our spirit man), Holy Spirit, and wisdom of the ages. We worship the Father in spirit and in truth. This book illustrates how you use the five senses to access the kingdom of God and gives you instruction on what to do to come into the presence of the Lord. To those who are hungry and thirsty, this will be an answer to your prayer. I highly encourage you to read *School of the Supernatural* because the supernatural should be natural for the saints.

BOB JONES

Not only does *School of the Supernatural* give greater detail about accessing the kingdom of God through your five natural senses, it explores the possibilities of living in the presence of God by experiencing Heaven's realm on earth and not being bound by our soul. It explains the supernatural lifestyle Christians are entitled to now, not when they die. It's a must-read book that will whet your spiritual appetite for more of the supernatural realm.

BONNIE JONES

Ryan Wyatt is as real as they come! I have both known Ryan, and have ministered with him for many years now and have witnessed powerful demonstrations and key revelations of Kingdom power and authority in his life.

Ryan's new book *The School of the Supernatural* is packed full of practical revelation knowledge that will unlock your understanding on how to move in the supernatural graces of God. Ryan also has an incredible ability as a revelatory teacher to make living in the supernatural easy to comprehend. This new book, *School of the Supernatural,* will feed you or your own school with practical insights and revelation for a long, long time to come! I highly recommend anyone who is hungering and thirsting for more of the manifest Presence of Jesus to get this book and devour the contents!

JEFF JANSEN
Founder, Global Fire Ministries International
Global Fire Church & World Miracle Center, Murfreesboro TN
Author, *Glory Rising* and *Glory Rising Manual*

This book presents a balanced, unapologetic case in favor of the supernatural realities available to us. You will be stirred to awaken your senses to experience God in the routines of your daily lives... and then some!

ALBERTO & KIMBERLY RIVERA

I have known Ryan for nine years. Ryan brings a level of credibility to the supernatural realm. Ryan writes as one who has experienced all that he conveys. This book will not only inform you but also bring you to experience the reality of the supernatural realm.

TREVOR BAKER
Senior Leader of the Apostolic Resource Centre
Dudley, UK

School of the Supernatural challenges and equips you to live a supernatural life, naturally. Ryan's testimonies will impart supernatural faith and lead you into personal encounters with God and His Glory. Join him on his journey to discover Jesus' ever-present eternal kingdom and bring Heaven on earth.

CHÉ AHN
Senior Pastor, HRock Church
President, Harvest International Ministry
International Chancellor, Wagner Leadership Institute

Ryan represents a new breed of fiery revivalists who are giving language to the aching hearts of a generation longing to experience a very real and supernatural God. Dive into this book, devour the language, and step into a greater measure of operating and releasing the supernatural in your own life.

SEAN FEUCHT
Founder, Burn 24/7
Author, *Fire and Fragrance*

Ryan Wyatt offers passionate and practical insight that is extremely valuable for believers today. Readable, instructive, and packed with weighty concepts, this insightful book will sharpen your ability to lead a spiritual life. I highly recommend *School of the Supernatural* as a guide to teach us how to become naturally supernatural.

LARRY RANDOLPH
Larry Randolph Ministries

Ryan Wyatt is that rare quality of individual who is a burning light in his generation. He combines illumination with fire, and changes whatever atmosphere he comes into contact with.

LANCE WALLNAU

Contents

Authentic Christianity
Is Supernatural

Every human being was created to be naturally supernatural and to interact with the supernatural realm. This is something you will more deeply understand after reading this book. This reality has caused many believers in Jesus Christ to "shy away" from anything supernatural because many of us have seen the abuses and deceptions and counterfeits of the supernatural in the world around us, in areas such as the New Age Movement, Occultism, or even in Hollywood.

I've written this book for a few reasons. First off, I want to set the record straight for Christians and show you that it is your biblical right and even "responsibility" to interact with God in a supernatural lifestyle. Second, I want you to see that there is an authentic supernatural lifestyle available for those who follow Jesus Christ and then there is a counterfeit supernatural, that has been instigated by satan. Third, this book will launch you into a journey of actually learning "how to" live in a supernatural lifestyle and relationship with God.

Every human being was created with what I call a "God-shaped hole" in his or her heart, and it can only be filled by the reality of God. Many Christians, at one time, had an awesome salvation encounter with God but were then only introduced to corporate church meetings. Going to church is great and all believers should be committed to a local church. However, the foundation of Christianity is a real, authentic, experiential relationship with God. Many people are taught about God but never really taught how to interact with and experience God on a daily basis. God is completely supernatural and He is experienced in supernatural ways. It is the highest calling of every human being to be brought back into a life-giving, earth-impacting, experientially supernatural relationship with God.

Is that the cry of your heart? Do you want more out of your relationship with God? Do you want to experience the realities of God like you read about in the Bible? Those biblical stories and realities are still available for you and I today. You were never called to serve an "idea" of God, or a "form" of God. You have been called into the most fulfilling, exciting, thrilling relationship that humanity has ever dreamed of. A supernatural relationship with God! Read on and learn how.

Chapter 1

What Is Authentic Supernatural Christianity?

Years ago, I experienced a visitation from the Lord that began a paradigm shift for me. I was in a hotel room by myself when suddenly the temperature of the room changed, becoming very, very warm. I went to check the thermostat, but the furnace was not even on. Suddenly, the fear of the Lord gripped me and I felt His tangible presence. I went and sat down. I began to weep and to vibrate from the inside out. It felt very different from other vision-type encounters I have had. I became aware that He was coming—literally coming—into the room.

Immediately, Jesus walked in from around the corner of my room, and He walked right up to me. He was dripping with oil from head to toe. As He came and stood next to me (where I was working hard just to stay in my chair), some of the oil came off onto me. I remember sitting there wiping my clothes and oil was on them, wiping my hair and oil was on it, wiping my face and oil was all over it.

He spoke. He said, "Ryan, this is the oil of the overcomer. I am releasing it in this hour for those who will begin to position themselves for it." Then He went on to say, "I am desperately hungry that I would have a people who will lay hold of their full inheritance. . . . I and I alone am your inheritance. . . . I and I alone am to be your possession" (see Ezek. 44:28).

Jesus also said to me, "I am desperately hungry that I would have my full inheritance in my people." For the first time, I really began to understand the fact that Jesus has an inheritance as well. His inheritance is not just born-again believers. He took me to the third chapter of Ephesians where Paul was speaking about the Church, how *"the manifold wisdom of God might be made known by the church to the principalities and powers in the heavenly places"* (Eph. 3:10 NKJV). The "manifold wisdom of God" refers to all of who God is—His character, His love, His presence, and His power. Through the Church, He wants to display all of who He is, so that the powers of darkness will be overcome by His Light.

That is His inheritance. Jesus will not have a beat-up, bruised, and broken-but-saved Bride who will join Him someday in Heaven. He will have a powerful, victorious, effective warrior Bride who is demonstrating the victory won by Jesus on the Cross and who is occupying and advancing the Kingdom until He comes again.

Journey Toward Our Full Inheritance

That experience awakened me to the grand plan of God with His people in the earth. I realized that He is coming to pour out fresh oil upon our lives so that we will be overcomers in the times that we are living in. In John 16:33, Jesus said, *"Behold in this world you will have tribulation, but take heart, for I have overcome the world."* Even in the midst of the worst storms of life, it was like Jesus carried His own weather system with Him. It didn't matter what kind of oppressive type of atmosphere He walked into, Jesus could bring Heaven to that atmosphere and He could change the atmosphere rather than bowing a knee to it. He is raising up His people on the earth to be "overcomers." His Bride, His Body, His Church will be the ones who are 100 percent sold out to Him, feeding upon His goodness and fullness as their inheritance, and then weathering every storm that comes their way as they demonstrate the goodness and power of God to the world!

His People Arising Out From the Religious World System

Ezekiel 44 is one of the Bible passages that Jesus spoke to me in the visitation I mentioned above. I believe this passage prophetically speaks to us about what is happening in our time. God was speaking to Ezekiel about two kinds of priests. One kind of priest was serving God with their lips and their heads but not with their hearts. Their faithfulness to the Lord had evaporated and they were leading others astray. God said something to Ezekiel that is frightening and eye-opening for our times. God said He would allow those "priests" to continue ministering, but they would not come near to Him.

Then God speaks to Ezekiel about another kind of priest, the Zadok Priesthood. These priests worshiped God with their hearts, and not just their heads, and they remained faithful to Him. Therefore, God says the Zadok Priesthood would be allowed free and open access into His most holy place. This speaks of experiencing the very glory of God. God goes on to tell Ezekiel that through the Zadok Priesthood, the world would once again discern the difference between the holy and the profane, or unholy.

I believe this is happening in our times today as well. As God is increasingly pouring out His glory and advancing His Kingdom, a separation is taking place. God's glory brings unity amongst those who are seeking His glory, but it brings division amongst everyone else. Jesus was the manifestation of God's glory when He walked the earth, and He brought a dividing line of decision everywhere He went. It is the same today. God's people are beginning to come out and arise out of the "religious system" of our day. There is a religious system that includes all the religions of the world, including Christianity. Jesus never came to birth a religion, and that includes Christianity. He came to birth a family on the earth. He came to birth and produce His Bride! There are many who exist within the religion of Christianity who do not even know God. They are not born again and are attending churches that do not preach the Gospel. I know this because I have heard the testimony of many who have attended certain churches for years, yet never heard how to be saved.

You could say that there is a Church within the church. God's people, His Church, exists within the religious organization called the church. As God's glory continues to pour out upon the earth, His people are arising out of the dust of the world and its religious systems and are rallying around a movement of authentic supernatural Christianity. God's church is arising!

When the Kingdom of God comes, it shakes everything that can be shaken. God is pulling a remnant out of what we call the organizational Church. He is pulling out a remnant of those who are truly born again and going after Him and living for Him. He is pulling out that remnant; He is beginning to place His glory on them. And whenever the glory comes, it causes a rift. His glory is supernatural, and any time something supernatural happens, it causes controversy. But Jesus said, "I want a people who lay hold of their full inheritance." And when His people begin to lay hold of their full inheritance, He begins to obtain His. Like the Zadok Priesthood, God's people will arise in the earth; and by displaying His glory, the church will demonstrate to the world what is God and what is not God, what is holy and what is profane.

Awakening and Reformation

A new awakening and reformation is taking place in the church right now. God still speaks to people today. God still moves in supernatural ways, just as He did in the Old Testament; it is not flakey; it is not nutty. God is still supernatural. For the most part, you will never live a supernatural lifestyle or have supernatural encounters with God if you choose not to agree with that. God does not force things down people's throats. Sometimes He surprises people whether they like it or not; most of the time He doesn't. Most of the time you will experience the kinds of things in your life that you have opened yourself up to believe for.

The glory of God still invades earth. The things that happened in the Bible still happen. Our participation in all of this depends not only on our willingness, but also to a large extent on our ability to comprehend His ways. We need to learn the language of the Spirit and the culture of the Kingdom of God. We need other believers around us—and a book like this one—to school us in the ways of a supernatural God. God's people are arising, and Jesus' inheritance is maturing.

Jesus' Inheritance—a Mature Church/Bride

God wants to have a body of people who have entered into the fullness of the stature of the maturity of Christ, the unity of the faith, and the full intimate knowledge of the Son of God, who grow up into Him who is the Head (see Eph. 4:13). He wants to have a body on the earth that is proportionate in maturity to Himself as the Head that is in Heaven.

We are going to be victorious. And that is Jesus' inheritance. In Ephesians 3 verses 7-13, Paul said there is a mystery that has been hidden for ages. Paul says, *"People in times past have tried to understand this mystery, but by God's grace, he has revealed it to me and I am going to shine some light on it for you."* He says that through the church the manifold wisdom of God, all of who God is, the manifold nature of God, God himself, through the church God is going to display who He is, display His greatness, display His manifold wisdom to the principalities and the powers of the air.

It is not enough that Jesus paid the price and has won the victory for us. The victory has been paid for—but it has not been collected on. It has not been enforced. It has been paid for, and it belongs to Him and to us. His inheritance is to have a body of people on the earth, His DNA on the earth, His family in the earth that will enforce the victory over the enemy and begin to demonstrate the manifold wisdom of God, right in the face of the principalities and powers of the air. That is His inheritance. Jesus' inheritance is completely tied up in the "success" of His people. This is why Jesus will not come back for a beat-up, bruised, broken bride. He will be released to come back from Heaven at that time when the Father looks down upon the earth and sees a mature Bride/Body, operating in the same stature of maturity that Jesus walked in when He walked the earth. The Father will then release Jesus to return and claim His inheritance. Jesus, as the Head in Heaven, will return and rest upon His mature corporate Body/Bride and rule and reign on the earth with them.

The Supernatural Is Not a Fad

In the time of Jesus' earthly ministry, the religious people of that day rejected Him. They rejected Jesus because they had expected Him to come in a certain way and He didn't. When He came in a way that broke their box and their idea of how He would come, they rejected Him. Would the Church today reject Him as well? Absolutely, yes. In many circles that is happening. Many people who are legitimately born-again and legitimately love God just do not want anything to do with anything that is supernatural because it seems "weird" to them. The supernatural is a very controversial thing.

We need to realize that the supernatural is not a fad. It is not a new trend; it is not something that's here today and gone tomorrow. The supernatural is part of the DNA of the Gospel of the Kingdom, and if you are a born-again believer in Jesus Christ, *you are supernatural*. You cannot escape this dimension of God and this dimension of who you are in Him.

Now, that does not guarantee that you are operating or living in the supernatural. Our traditions have put restrictions on us, limits on what we can expect to experience in God. The Bible and God do not put these limits on us. Yes, there are boundaries or limits, but they are much, much more broad and vast than the theological boxes that many of us have been trained and raised up in. I want to say right up front that you can be normal, you can be grounded in the Word of God, you can have good character, you can operate in wisdom, *and* you can be phenomenally supernatural. That is difficult for many leaders to accept.

Jesus was labeled as a cult leader. He said hard-to-believe things, such as "You are going to eat my flesh and drink my blood" (see John 6:55-56). I'm not sure how much more extreme we could get. Many of His disciples and His followers left. These were people who were on the same page with Jesus. They were not like the other religious people, the Pharisees and Sadducees that initially rejected Jesus. These were ones who received Jesus. But when Jesus wanted to introduce more revelation to them, they decided to turn away. Does this sound familiar? This is what many are doing in the church today as God is trying to teach us to live supernaturally. People once received amazing revelations of God but then decided to camp around those revelations and not move on with the cloud as God reveals more about Himself. This is how many denominations have formed all over the world.

The cloud of God came to restore truths that had been lost during the Dark Ages. During the Dark Ages, so much revelation was lost that by the time Martin Luther nailed his ninety-five theses to the door of the church in Wittenberg, it was a major revolution and a revelation that you could even be saved by faith and grace. Throughout the centuries, God has been restoring truth to us. In just about every outpouring of His Spirit that has come, some truth of the Kingdom has been restored.

Jesus said, "I have come to seek and save that which was lost" (see Luke 19:10). When Jesus said that, He was not just talking about lost humanity. Jesus was also talking about the Kingdom. Adam and Eve lost more than just that deep level of glory relationship with God; they also lost the Kingdom that rested upon them, that they carried in the earth. That is why Jesus said, *"the Kingdom of heaven is at hand"* (Matt. 3:2). He brought the Kingdom back to earth. And since then, the cloud of God has come to restore more Kingdom truths.

Martin Luther restored the truth of being saved by faith and grace. The cloud of God visited John Wesley and gave him a revelation of "holiness of heart and life" that was substantiated by Scripture. What Luther and Wesley said made church leaders nervous, because it was not in their understanding of Scripture, but it is a good thing most of our forefathers and foremothers were open to the new revelation and they did not reject it. The Methodists formed around John Wesley, but the Cloud wanted to move further. God never intends us to leave these great revelations behind, but He also never intended us to camp around them forever. God wants us to make those scriptural revelations a part of our lives and continue to progress and move forward as God reveals more to us from His Word. God's cloud, so to speak, is still moving today. We have had all these moves of justification by faith, holiness, evangelism, the prophetic, the apostolic, healing and miracles, and more.

With every one of these revelations, the Body did not leave the previous revelations behind. Taken together, everything that God has restored makes us more full Gospel believers. I believe there is a lot of the Gospel of the Kingdom that God wants to restore to us. God at this time is also moving toward restoring the reality of the supernatural to the Body of Christ. Some people are accepting and some are not.

Well-meaning people have said to me, "Ryan, why can't you just get people saved, heal the sick, and move into miracles? That's okay, but leave the supernatural out of it." Pastors have told me, behind the scenes, "Ryan, the anointing that I have on my life today came because of supernatural moments where God's glory touched my life in a tangible way. A grace came into my life and I began to move in words of knowledge and miracles." What shocked me was their next statement. The next thing that some of these leaders said was, "…but I will not open that up to the people that I lead."

And I said "Why? If it had such profound impact on your life, why won't you open it up?"

Their response was, "Because it is too hard to pastor." It seems to me that by its very nature, the fivefold ministry of apostles, prophets, evangelists, pastors, and teachers (see Eph. 4:11) requires that your number-one call is to equip the saints for the work of ministry. True authority comes when you actually serve the body to be equipped in ministry. The reality is that babies "mess themselves"! It is the same way with people learning to grow in the things of God's Spirit. Yes, it can be messy. Yes, people will make mistakes. But this is why we have the Bible as our foundation of truth and we have godly leaders as accountability in people's lives. We must not hinder people from learning to interact with God on a supernatural level. God once called *all* of Israel to the base of the mountain to experience His glory. But the people told Moses to experience the glory himself and give them the words of God. May it not be so today. Yes, God still uses leadership in His church, but as leaders, we are supposed to be leading people into a real, tangible, foundational, experiential, supernatural lifestyle with God! We must continue moving with the cloud and "embrace" the revelations that God is revealing to us from His Word concerning living a supernatural lifestyle.

What Is Authentic Supernatural Christianity?

Each one of us is meant to live a lifestyle of direct encounter with a supernatural God. Daniel 11:32 says, *"But the people who know their God shall be strong and carry out great exploits"* (NKJV). Another version says that *"The people who know their God shall stand firm and take action"* (ESV). Either way it means the same thing.

In John 5 verses 39-40, Jesus says, *"You search the scriptures, for in them you think you have eternal life. And these are they which testify of me but you are not willing to come to me that you may have life"* (NKJV). So, authentic Christianity is more than a head knowledge of the Scriptures. It's allowing the Bible to lead you into a life-giving, dynamic relationship with God.

The first element of authentic supernatural Christianity is complete love and devotion to God. Number two is that those people who are living in that secret place of love and devotion with God will bring the realm of Heaven to earth daily. I say "daily," because this is a lifestyle. Evangelism is not an event; Christianity is not a Sunday-morning event. Your life with God is a day-to-day lifestyle and it is bringing the realm of Heaven to earth daily and destroying the works of the devil (see 1 John. 3:8). It is touching God daily and then undoing the works of the devil in the earthly realm.

The Priestly Lifestyle— Wholehearted Lovers of God

Earlier in my walk with God, I had a visionary experience with the Lord where He stood before me with a hot, fresh loaf of bread in one hand and a scepter in the other. He told me to choose one. I knew that the scepter represented power and authority and I wanted to do great things for the Kingdom, so I reached for the scepter. As I did, Jesus pulled back the scepter and extended the fresh bread to me. He said this: "I will not release overcoming kings until I first have consecrated priests." This launched a season of my life where God began to teach me what authentic supernatural Christianity really is and how God sets the priorities in our lives.

As believers, each of us is called to live a priestly lifestyle and a kingly lifestyle. However, in order to live in the authority and power of the kingly lifestyle, we must first learn to live the consecrated priestly lifestyle. The Bible says we are the "royal priesthood" of God (see 1 Pet. 2:9).

Don't get caught up with the word "priest," because I am not referring to the modern-day Catholic priests or other kinds of priests. I'm talking about each believer being a priest in the royal priesthood, which is the Church. Like the Old Testament priesthood, we are called out from everyone else, called to live a different kind of lifestyle. Everything about Old Testament priests was to be "unto the Lord." Their work was unto the Lord. Their service was unto the Lord. Their relationships were consecrated and dedicated to the Lord.

As a tribe of people, they were called out to become mediators between Heaven and earth. If the rest of Israel wanted to encounter God and His glory, they came to the priests. Today, if people want to encounter God, they come to one of the followers of Jesus, each of whom is a temple for the Spirit of God. The Old Testament priests would take the sacrifices and offer them up to the Lord for the forgiveness of sins. The fire of the glory of God would come at times and consume the sacrifice. You can see how this parallels the way it works now with today's royal priesthood, the Church. For the most part, if the world is going to encounter God, then they will see and encounter God through His people, the Church. We, as the Church, owe the world an encounter with His goodness, glory, and power!

Being a priest, either an Old Testament or a New Testament one, requires a lifestyle of consecration. Priests cannot live like everyone else. And that points to a big problem we have today. We have many people, thousands and thousands of people, who have been born again and who have committed themselves to a church, but they are not living the lifestyle of a true New Testament royal priesthood. There is a significant difference between being committed to Church culture and being a bondservant of Jesus Christ.

Once you are born again, if you want to lay hold of all the promises that God has already paid for you to lay hold of, you are going to have to labor and fight and be transformed in order to grow up in them. Yes, Jesus has paid the price already and everything He has paid for is given to us freely, by His grace. However, there is a daily laboring that is required in order to position ourselves to receive of what He provides to us freely.

There is a difference between having Christ in you, the hope of glory, being regenerated and born again, having the seed of the Kingdom in you, but then also having Christ "fully formed in you." There is a difference. There is a process. You may be saved and guaranteed for Heaven, bound for Heaven, committed to a church, and all of those kinds of things, but you also have acquired an enemy who is going to fight you tooth and nail every single day. He will try to do everything he can to prevent you from operating in your priestly anointing and laying hold of all that God has for you.

Jesus says, *"Do not labor for the food that perishes but for the food that endures to eternal life which the Son of Man will give, for on him God the Father has set His seal"* (John 6:27 NKJV). Then He goes on to say, *"I am the bread of life; he who comes to Me will not hunger, and he who believes in Me will never thirst"* (John 6:35 NASB). Jesus is like the manna that came down from Heaven and we can receive Him freely. But He says that there is a labor involved in order to eat of that bread. The priestly lifestyle is hard work, because it means fighting through the tactics of the enemy as he comes against you in your day-to-day life.

Kingdom priests are committed to their King and to their battle, not only when they see a breakthrough or when they feel the grace of God flowing into their lives. They are committed to God when they do not feel like it, when it feels like work, when it feels like sacrifice, when persecution is involved, when they are misunderstood. Old Testament priests, after all, were covered in blood. That is a prophetic picture. They were mediators of Heaven and earth, but there was sacrificial work involved.

The first thing God is looking for before He starts granting you higher levels of authority in the kingly lifestyle is that you learn how to be a consecrated priest. Galatians 4:1 tells us that even though you are a child of God and an heir of God, and therefore the master of everything...if you are still a child, it is as if you are a slave. If a king has a son, and the son is the heir, he is the one who will own and administer everything the king possesses. But when he is still a little child, he does not understand those responsibilities, and doesn't yet have any commitment to it. A good king and father would only give more authority, responsibility, and power to His son as he matures and becomes more consecrated to the King and the Kingdom.

In the church, we wonder why God does not seem to be moving through us in power, why does He not use us more often for miracles, signs, and wonders. All believers can move in power and heal the sick, but it will happen in a much more consistent and powerful way as we become more consecrated to Him out of love, in the priestly lifestyle.

True consecration is when every area of your life is truly dedicated to the Lord first and foremost. In everything you do, you think about the Lord first. You are seeking first the kingdom and His righteousness in everything that you do, and no part of your life is exempt (see Matt. 6:33). You are pursuing His will and His wisdom and you are able to obey Him better all the time because His Spirit is transforming you from the inside out.

The last thing I want to mention about the priestly lifestyle is that it is one that is lived "wholeheartedly" before the Lord, from a place of intense love and fascination with God. New Testament priests and believers are those who consecrate their lives to the Lord, not because of duty, but because of love! They labor daily for one thing, and that is to gaze upon the beauty of the Lord and to feast upon His goodness. Priests are those who do not obey the Lord out of fear or threat of negative consequences, but they obey the Lord out of affection for Him. The priestly lifestyle is one of laid-down surrender because you've tasted of the goodness of God and have found that there is nothing else like our God in all the earth!

People who live in this way, in the priestly lifestyle, will be the ones who live a supernatural lifestyle, full of the glory of God. They will be the ones who experience deep intimacy with the Lord, and experience His presence in a very real way. These people will be the ones who literally carry and manifest the substance of who God is to the world around them. They will be the ones who operate in the authority and power of the Kingdom as they demonstrate a kingly lifestyle.

The Kingly Lifestyle—Destroying the Works of the Devil

So, we see that the first element of authentic supernatural Christianity is living the priestly lifestyle of wholehearted passion and love for God, in a supernatural lifestyle. The second element of supernatural Christianity is the kingly lifestyle. As we saw above, Daniel 11:32 says, *"But the people who know their God shall be strong and carry out great exploits."* This is the two-fold expression of authentic Christianity. The priestly lifestyle of truly and intimately "knowing our God" and the kingly lifestyle of "being strong and doing great exploits."

The kingly lifestyle is one of demonstrating the goodness and power of God and His Kingdom. The natural byproduct of living an intimate priestly lifestyle is that the substance of God will be a fragrance upon your life that others experience. When others around you experience the presence, power, and goodness of God from your life, then the works of darkness begin to be unraveled in their lives! We read in First John 3:8 that the reason the Son of God appeared was to destroy the works of the devil. The natural byproduct of intimacy with Jesus is that He begins to live through you and destroy the works of the devil in your life and in the lives of those you impact. Again, the kingly lifestyle is all about laying hold of God and demonstrating Him to the world around you by acts of love, goodness, and power.

Jesus Christ—The Perfect Prototype

Jesus perfectly modeled authentic supernatural Christianity for us during His earthly life. He perfectly modeled the priestly and kingly lifestyle, and as He did so, He demonstrated the will of the Kingdom of God, on earth as it is in Heaven.

When Jesus came to the earth in human flesh, He came to be an exact prototype of what is possible for every born-again believer. Jesus was what you would call the pattern Son. He came to pattern, to show a model for us. Jesus Christ lived in two realms, or two worlds, at one time. Everything He did on earth was out of an intimate relationship with the Father and Holy Spirit. That is not the kind of life we see today in the church at large. We are in the middle of a movement of the restoration of authentic supernatural Christianity.

The Bible says in John 1:14 that *"the Word became flesh and dwelt* [or tabernacled] *among us, and we have seen his glory."* This was Jesus. Jesus, the Son of God, tabernacled Himself in human flesh and demonstrated through His life the very glory of God to this earth. The Bible also says that Jesus was the firstborn among many brothers (see Rom. 8:29), and that He was the Last Adam (see 1 Cor. 15:45). Jesus came as a new Adam, the last Adam, a new prototype of a new kind of people. Every born-again person is no longer of the line of the first Adam, but rather of the line of the Last Adam, Jesus Christ. As believers, we are a new breed in the earth. We are the most supernatural "organism" (not "organization") and the most supernatural people existing in the earth. We are God's people.

We are the royal priesthood. We are His holy nation that exists right in the midst of the other nations of this world (see 1 Pet. 2:9). We are His vessels. We are His habitation.

Just as Jesus tabernacled Himself in human flesh and manifested the glory of God during His earthly life, born-again believers are now inhabited by God. God has now tabernacled Himself within all those that call Him their Lord and God and have welcomed Him into their hearts and spirits. God now dwells within His people, and just as Jesus did, we now carry the mandate to manifest the goodness and glory of God to the entire world!

The Cry of a Supernatural People

There is a cry arising from the hearts of God's people on the earth today, similar to what arose from Moses' heart on the mountain of God. In Exodus 33, Moses voiced his heart by imploring God not to send them out unless He was going to be in their midst. Moses asked that God's presence would be with them. Moses said, "God, how shall it be known among the nations of the earth that we are Your people unless Your presence goes with us?" (see Exod. 33:16). Moses knew that it was only the presence and glory of God that would make them distinct from all other people. Then Moses cried out to God and said, "God, show me your ways and show me your glory!"

As you read on in this book, I am going to teach you some of the ways of God, as revealed to us in Scripture, and in moments when I experienced His glory. As God's people, His Church, we cannot go on living with merely a head knowledge or elementary level experiential knowledge of God. We must advance and move forward, deeper into God's glory, being transformed from one degree of glory to another degree of glory. His supernatural glory will make us distinct from any other people, and the world will see His glory!

Now, let's move on as we come to understand that we were created to be *naturally supernatural....*

Chapter 2

Created to Be Naturally Supernatural

God created you and me to have the capacity to live as multidimensional persons. But most of us do not live that way. By default, we live in the physical "body" dimension, and we take our directions from our minds and emotions, which represent the dimension we call "soul." We pay only limited attention to our spirits, which limits our daily life to the material world.

Your human spirit is your connection with God. His Spirit communicates with your spirit. Therefore, it is important to learn about the three-part nature of human life—spirit, soul, and body—if we have a desire to walk with our supernatural God. In this chapter, I want to give you some teaching on the purpose of living in the supernatural, and a bigger picture of what God is trying to do other than just opening us up to supernatural encounters. Because there *is* a bigger picture. I mean, supernatural encounters are awesome, but the number one purpose for them is intimacy with God, and then after intimacy with Him, God has a purpose for us. God has a mission for you and me and I want you to be able to follow Him into it. I want you to see that it is not just about having a supernatural lifestyle or encounters with God; it is about the fact that if we do not learn to live a supernatural lifestyle with God, then we cannot fulfill the mandate that we have, a call from God that we have on the earth. Apart from living in the supernatural, we cannot be Jesus Christ's inheritance and fulfill the call to manifest God to the principalities and powers of the air. So we must learn to live out of our spirits, if we intend to live supernatural lives.

The Three-Part Nature of Humans

Do you have a computer? Do you know how to operate every single function of that computer? If so, then you are a master of that computer. Otherwise, you are limited to only those functions that you understand.

In the same way, we need to understand that humans were created to be three parts: spirit, soul, and body. If we do not understand the functions of the spirit part of our nature, the soul part of our nature, and the body part of our nature, then we are not going to be able to effectively live in the supernatural.

We also need to understand that every single one of these three parts was damaged at the Fall of humanity, with Adam and Eve. Your spirit was damaged, your soul was damaged, and your body was damaged. And one of the bigger purposes of God is restoration. He is restoring His people, His kingdom, His representation on earth. In the current period of restoration, God is working to restore us, not just in spirit, which starts with being born again, but in our souls as well. One day, born-again believers will receive glorified bodies, and then the effects of the Fall on our bodies will be completely reversed as well. When all is said and done, we are going to be people whose spirits, souls, and bodies are completely restored and whole. We will be able to function as Adam and Eve did before the Fall, at liberty in our spirits, souls, and bodies.

The apostle Paul wrote to the Thessalonian believers: *"May the God of peace himself sanctify you completely."* And the verse continues: *"…and may your whole spirit and soul and body be preserved blameless at the coming of our Lord Jesus Christ"* (1 Thess. 5:23 NKJV). As human beings, we can access a lot of the maturity and somewhat of the fullness of being restored spirit, soul, and even some in the body on this side of eternity before receiving glorified bodies. God has given human beings an incredible capacity to manifest the glory of God on this side of eternity.

Adam and Eve were incredibly supernatural. Some theologians say that the Garden was hundreds of miles around, yet Adam and Eve tended the whole thing. How do you think they did that? Was it by walking? You know, I think we are going to be surprised, one day when we are fully restored, spirit, soul, and body; we will be able to operate fully in the spirit realm under the administration of Jesus ruling and reigning in the earth, and we'll be able to travel throughout the nations of the world as quick as a thought. We will be able to do things in the spirit just like angels do now, since we will not have the limitations that we currently have in our bodies because of the Fall.

We need to learn how to operate in the fullness of who God has called us to be. Let's look at Genesis 2 verse 7 (ESV): *"Then the Lord God formed the man of dust from the ground,"* [that's the first element, your body, which has your five natural senses] *"and breathed into his nostrils the breath of life"* [that is your spirit man, your human spirit] *"and then the man became a living creature"* [and that word *creature* is a soul, a living soul]. So when the body and spirit came together, the third element was created as well, which is the soul.

Now I want to just hit on some different teachings that people have on this topic. A lot of people teach what is called the dualistic belief when it comes to soul and body. In other words, they believe that we are *not* "tripartite" (which means we have three parts: spirit, soul, and body) but that we are dualistic, with just a body and then a spirit/soul combination. They say that our spirit and our soul are the same thing. This is a popular concept. But it is not accurate. It is not biblical.

Take, for example, Hebrews chapter 4 verse 12: *"For the word of God is living and active, sharper than any two-edged sword, piercing to the division of soul and of spirit, of joints and of marrow, and discerning the thoughts and intentions of the heart"* (ESV). The spirit and soul are the nonphysical, nonvisible parts of who we are. The body is a no-brainer. You do not have to try to understand it; you can see the body. But the spirit and the soul are not visible; they are deep within a person and they are a part of who you are and they are so intertwined that, especially when you are still a nonbeliever, you cannot tell them apart. Understand, there is a spirit in a nonbeliever. The spirit is what allows a person to operate in the spiritual realm, and unbelievers can operate in the spiritual realm.

Jesus said that He is the doorway: *"I am the way and the truth and the life"* (John 14:6). He said that anybody who enters in but by Him is a thief and a robber (see John 10:1). He didn't say you couldn't enter into the spirit realm; you cannot enter into the Kingdom, but you can enter into the spirit realm. So that means they are operating in spirit realm dimensions illegally and outside of the parameters that God set up for us, which is through Jesus Christ.

It's not only unbelievers that fail to differentiate between their souls and spirits. Many believers, once becoming born again, can't tell the difference either, and they are still pretty much run and dominated by their soul life. This is why we still have a lot of fleshly, carnal Christians. It's possible to be completely redeemed in spirit and love God and have a born-again experience and continue to live according to your *old* man. Paul even warned believers many times not to do that.

You can live dominated by your flesh and you can live dominated by your soul and your own wants and your own desires, but as you learn to hear the voice of God and as you learn to find God within you, you will learn what your spirit man feels like. You learn what it feels like when you have tapped into your spirit and you are operating from the dimensions of your human spirit, because that is where God lives. When believers are born again,

God comes and mingles and merges with their spirits and He regenerates their spirits. First Corinthians 6:17 tells us that *"he who is joined to the Lord becomes one spirit with him"* (ESV).

But then many believers go on for the rest of their Christian life not maturing in the things of the spirit. When you are born as a baby you learn to eat, you learn to talk, and you learn to use all your natural senses and you develop in them. Many believers can't even feel their spirit and can't even feel the operation of God within them because they became Christians, joined a church, and they think that is all there is. They could be a believer for 30 or 40 years and still their spirit man remains like a baby. This happens all the time. Most believers can't tell the difference between when they are operating from their soul or operating out of their spirit.

The writer of Hebrews described the two-edged, spirit/soul-dividing sword of the Word for a good reason. *"For the word of God is living and active, sharper than any two edged sword, piercing to the division of soul and of spirit, of joints and of marrow, and discerning the thoughts and intentions of the heart"* (ESV). A living, active, spoken word of God in your life causes a separation to take place between your soul and spirit, so that you notice the difference. That passage mentions joints and marrow and there is an interesting reason for this. When the Old Testament priests were preparing to sacrifice animals, the Lord had commanded that every single part of the animal be exposed to the open. The point of it was that this is a prophetic picture of the way God sees everything. No matter how hard you try and hide it, God sees it. So He instructed them to expose every single part of the animal, even to the point where they had this little knife to jab it into the bones of the animal so they could open up the bones and even the bone marrow would be exposed. By analogy, we can see that the soul and the spirit are completely intertwined, like bone and marrow, but there is as much of a difference between spirit and soul as between bone and marrow—and only the living, active word of God can show you the difference between the two.

The word of God is living and active. Jesus said, *"the words that I speak to you are spirit and they are life"* (John 6:63). That verse does not refer to the written Word of God as much as it refers to every time Jesus speaks to you. The words that He speaks have spirit to them, tangible substance; they have life in them. There was something about Jesus. When He spoke, He captivated people. He was a man who lived in another realm. When He spoke, people were amazed. They would say "who is this man that speaks with such authority?" (See Matt. 7:29; Mark 1:22,27.)

Adopting a Hebrew Mindset

Some people say, "We are a spirit, we have a soul, and we live in a body." Have you heard that before? Other people have been taught the opposite: "No, we are a soul and we have a spirit and we live in a body." Both of those teachings are a product of our Western way of thinking, this worldview in which we compartmentalize everything.

The Bible was written by people from the East and it expresses an Eastern way of thinking, specifically, the Hebrew mindset. The Hebrew mindset did not compartmentalize everything. Not at all. Never, in any of the writings or the teachings of the culture of that day, would they have said that we are a spirit that has a soul that lives in the body, or that we are a soul that has a spirit that lives in the body. They looked at the whole person as being spirit, soul, and body. To them, it was not as if we are a spirit and we can do without the soul. No, they were sure of it: you are spirit *and* soul *and* body. So much so that if you were to remove one of those elements, you would cease to exist as a full person.

In fact, for all of eternity you are always going to be spirit, soul, and body. When you get to Heaven, you are still going to have emotions, and you are going to have soul activity. You are still going to have personality. God's not going to have a bunch of robots. You are still going to have the capacity within you to give your emotions to God and worship Him. And you are still going to have a body, although it will be in its glorified form. Each and every human being is a three-part being: spirit and soul and body.

To illustrate what I mean, consider a three-story house. If you had a house that has three floors, the bottom floor would be like your body: it has the greatest point of access to the natural realm. The middle floor would be like your soul: that is your mind, your will, and your emotions. The top floor would be like your spirit: it has the most contact with God and the heavenly realm. If you took away one of those stories, you would no longer have a three-story house; it would cease to exist as a three-story house.

Another illustration would be the way the people of Israel set up their temple, at God's instruction. The Bible says that we are temples of the living God (see 1 Cor. 3:16). The Old Testament temple, God's temple, consisted of three compartments. It had the outer court, the inner court, and the holy of holies. We are the New Testament temples of God, and we are made up of three parts as well.

The outer court would represent your body. The outer court was outside under the sun. The inner court, which represents the human soul, came next. Then you have the holy of holies, which represents the part that is closest to the glory of God, closest to God himself; that is your spirit.

When God formed Adam from the dust of the ground, He was making a statement. He had a purpose in doing it that way. And this is obvious: the earth was his body. We are made of the earth. The reason God created man from the earth is because we are called to dominate and influence the earth with the Kingdom. Your earth suit, your body, gives you your five natural senses of seeing, hearing, smelling, touching, and tasting.

Then God breathed spirit into Adam. This was not the Holy Spirit. It was of the very essence of God that He breathed into Adam and formed his spirit man, a human spirit, within Adam. So when that spirit was breathed into you, you also were created of the heavenly realm. And that element of the spirit breathed into you has never had a beginning. In every human being is a part that has always existed. Even unregenerate, unsaved people have this part. That spirit that exists within every single human being has no beginning. Everything else you can think of in your life has had a beginning, except for God. God Himself has no beginning and no end. Before He created Heaven, He existed. Before He created angels, He existed. The One who always existed, who always was and always will be, took of that eternal essence and breathed it into you. Because of this reality, every single human being is created to live forever. You will live forever. The only question that remains on this issue for humanity is, "Will you choose to live forever with God or with satan?" That is a part of the Good News that we do not hear very often!

You can see the significance of this: the first element of Adam's creation came from the earth, and the second element of his creation came from God Himself, from the heavenly realm. Therefore, from the very beginning, humankind, created from two realms, is called to bring two realms together.

Functions of Your Spirit

Most of the time, outside of a sovereign move of God, if Heaven is going to touch earth and if the Kingdom is going to be demonstrated, it is going to require us hearing from God, being shown what to do, and having the guts to step out in the natural realm and act on it in obedience. It is not enough just to see it. To see it creates good prophetic conferences, but to act on it is a whole different thing. Many people hear the message but do not act on it. May God awaken us to the reality that this is our responsibility.

To both hear from God and then act on it, bringing Heaven to earth, requires the use of our spirit. The spirit relates to the spirit realm and it gives us God-consciousness. Since most believers do not even know they have a spirit, they have no contact with it. That is why so many believers feel they can't find God. Your spirit was created to contact, receive, and contain God. (For your personal study, here are just a few of many Scriptures in the Bible that refer to your human spirit: 1 Cor. 2:11; 1 Cor. 5:4; Rom. 8:16; 1 Cor. 14:14; 1 Cor. 14:32; Heb. 4:12; Heb. 12:23; Zech. 12:1; Prov. 20:27.)

The basic functions of your spirit include intuition, conscience, and communion with God. I will spend a paragraph describing each of these.

Intuition is another word for the sensing organ of the human spirit. Intuition involves a direct sensing, independent of any outside influence. It is that intuitive knowledge that comes to you without any help from your mind, will, or emotions. Your mind merely helps you to understand what you know through your intuition; your mind merely processes the information. Through intuition, the revelation of God and all the movements of the Holy Spirit can be made known to a believer.

In the Gospels, an incident is recounted in which Jesus actually rebuked some people based only on a spontaneous intuition, a sensing of the spirit within Him. In Mark chapter 2 verse 8, He said, "I sense or I perceive that you are reasoning thus and thus within you," and He rebuked people based on that. You and I may not be quite that confident, but our spiritual intuition is valid, and we can learn how to use it. (For your personal study: Matt. 26:41; Mark 2:8; Mark 8:12; John 11:33; Acts 20:22; 1 Cor. 2:11; 1 Cor. 16:18; 2 Cor. 7:13.)

The *conscience* is the discerning organ of the human spirit. The conscience distinguishes right and wrong, not through the influence of knowledge stored in the mind, but instead by a spontaneous direct judgment. Often, our reasoning will justify the things that our conscience judges. The work of the conscience is independent and direct. It does not bend to outside opinions. If someone should do wrong, it will raise its voice of accusation.

If you are a born-again believer, then your spirit's conscience has been awakened and reconnected to God. Your conscience tells you right and wrong because the Holy Spirit lives in your spirit. Many unbelievers retain a sense of conscience, but the more wicked they become in their life, the more covered up and more "seared," as the Bible says, their conscience becomes; so that the dividing lines between right and wrong become very blurred, to the point that what's good is called evil and what's evil is called good (see 1 Tim. 4:2). Those kinds of things happened in the Old Testament, and we are seeing an increase in these days. Things that were openly called evil by both believers and unbelievers just 20 or 30 years ago are today not only common but encouraged. (For your personal study: Deut. 2:30; Ps. 34:18; Ps. 51:10; John 13:21; Acts 17:16; Rom. 8:16; 1 Cor. 5:3; 2 Cor. 2:13; 2 Tim. 1:7.)

Communion, another function of your spirit, means worshiping God. The organs of your soul are incompetent to worship God. We especially use our emotions to worship

God, but true worship is in spirit and in truth (see John 4:23). God cannot be apprehended by our thoughts, our feelings, or our intentions. He can *only* be known directly in our spirits. Therefore, the worship of God and all of His communications to us happen directly in our spirits. Our minds, wills, and emotions of the soul simply process what first came by direct revelation to our spirits from the Holy Spirit. (For your personal study: Luke 1:47; John 4:23; Rom. 1:9; Rom. 7:6; Rom. 8:15-16; 1 Cor. 6:17; 1 Cor. 14:15-16; Rev. 21:10.)

Functions of Your Soul and Body

Briefly, that covers the primary functions of our spirits. Now, I want to describe the functions of the soul and also the body. The soul relates to the intellectual, emotional, and relational realm, or self-consciousness. Your soul is made up of your mind, your will, and your emotions. Many people call the soul the seat of human personality. We read in Genesis 2:7 that Adam's body was first created from the earth and then God breathed His very essence into him, which created his spirit. When the two came together, he *"became a living being"* (Gen. 2:7). Another word for it is "soul." In the King James Version and other versions of the Bible, people were so known by their souls that they would actually refer to people by the title of "soul" (see Gen. 12:5; Gen. 46:27 KJV).

But the basic functions of the soul are three: (1) *mind*—the instrument for thoughts, wisdom, knowledge, and reasoning; (2) *will*—the instrument for decisions and the power to choose; and (3) *emotion*—the instrument for expressing likes and dislikes. Many, many believers live in the soul realm, dominated by their own thoughts, their own wisdom, their own reasoning. Their will is their instrument for decisions, whether or not those decisions and choices are informed by the Spirit of God through their human spirit.

God created the soul to worship Him. God created the soul to be abandoned and devoted to Him. Therefore, emotion is part of our relationship with God. Some people say, "Well, we are not into emotional Christianity." But God *loves* emotional Christianity. He loves it when you spend your emotions on Him.

One of the reasons we need to understand and know the difference between our soul and our spirit is because we need to know, for example, when people are prophesying. Many times the first sentence or two is from God. But then people feel they have to carry it on and explain it. Sometimes the worst thing they can do is try to explain it. It is one thing to get the prophetic word; it is a whole different thing to learn how to deliver and interpret it. Interpreting the prophetic word may not be their job. Sometimes, because we do not understand the difference between soul and spirit, 80 percent of the word ends up becoming soulish and only 20 percent was really from God. Many believers do not discern when they have crossed the line. They do not discern when they have popped out of that sense of moving in the things of the Spirit into the arena of what "they" think about the prophetic word.

This does not just apply only to prophesying. This could apply to preaching, teaching, or anything else that requires the anointing of the Holy Spirit. Many people do many things in the name of the Holy Spirit, and many times, it is nothing but a work of the soul. We must learn the difference between what is originating from our human spirit, from the Holy Spirit, and what is originating from our soul.

One of the aspects of more mature sons and daughters of God is that their souls belong to God, not just their spirits. When you are born again, God comes and regenerates your spirit. He does not come and immediately restore your soul or take over your soul. Giving your soul and body to God is a lifelong process. Seeing God transform your soul takes work, faith, and belief. It is not as quick as salvation where God regenerates your spirit. This is why many believers who are not fully consecrated to God are dominated by their minds, their wills, and their emotions. When you are dominated by your mind, your will, and your emotions, and you have not fully given those things over to God, then even when you move in the gifts of the Spirit, they become tainted to some extent.

The function of your body is to relate to the physical and the earthly realm. Our five natural senses give us the capability of operating in the natural realm.

Naturally Supernatural

As you can see after reading this chapter, God created human beings to be naturally supernatural. He created us from two worlds, two realms, because we are called to be His agents to bring two worlds, two realms, together. We are called to partner with Jesus to fulfill the prayer of Matthew 6:9-10, that His Kingdom would come, on Earth as it is in Heaven!

Chapter 3

Becoming a Dwelling Place for God

We are in a time of restoration. *"In that he may send Jesus Christ who has preached to you before, whom Heaven must receive"* [That word "receive" actually means "retain"]. *"… until the times of restoration of all things which God has spoken by the mouth of all his holy prophets since the world began"* (Acts 3:20-21). Jesus is actually "retained" in the heavens until a restoration takes place on the earth.

Restoration of what? Many would say we are being restored back to what the Book of Acts church had, but I disagree. Think about it. We do not really want to go back to the Book of Acts, do we? The Book of Acts was the baby church. We like the miracles. We like the signs and the wonders. We like having 3,000 people being saved each day. We like the multitudes being added daily to the church. We want all those characteristics of the Book of Acts church to be restored to us today, but we should be asking God for much more than just being restored to where the Church was at its birth.

No, God is not restoring us to the Book of Acts. God is restoring us to before the Fall, to the Garden of Eden.

What is this restoration for? Why do we need to live in the supernatural? This chapter is going to first teach you about the original mandate given to humanity from God, and what God has always intended to do with us as His people. Then we will move on to how God's plan was sidetracked in the Garden of Eden by Adam and Eve's sin. This was no surprise to God. In the last chapter we learned about the makeup of humans as spirit, soul, and body. In this chapter, we will learn how each of those parts were damaged at the Fall and how God already had a plan in place to restore us in spirit, soul, and body; thereby restoring His kingdom, His glory, His habitation on the earth, through His people!

God wants a habitation on the earth, a place to dwell. A habitation is a body of people who are manifesting God in the earth just as Jesus did. But in order for that to happen we must be restored to that original mandate that was given to mankind. We must come into more of a divine union with God.

Disciples as Colonizers

You release whatever you become one with. If you become one with God, you release His goodness, power, love, and government wherever you go.

The Garden of Eden was God's original place of government on earth. Before the Fall, it was like Heaven and earth overlapped in the Garden. There was no curse on the earth, no sin, no death. Adam and Eve walked in the Garden in the cool of the day and the Lord would meet with them face-to-face and walk and talk with them. He told them, "Tend and keep the garden" (see Gen. 2:15). And He said, "I want you to be fruitful. I want you to multiply. I want you to have dominion and I want you to fill the earth" (see Gen. 1:26-28). Fill the earth with what? With their supernatural kingdom life-style, the place they were living. It represented the government of God.

If you look into the meaning of the word "garden," you will find that it comes from the word "cultivate," which is connected to the word "colony." When the Romans would colonize other areas, they would conquer an area and then they would set up a colony. Into that colony they would settle several hundred of their own people. Some were soldiers, some blacksmiths, some carpenters, some cooks. They were just everyday people, Roman citizens. The officials would put them in that colony and they would tell them, "You may be living in a distant foreign land, but we own it now. We want you to live as if you're in Rome. Dress like Romans. Eat like Romans. Maintain a Roman economy." And it worked. In one of those colonies, no matter where in the world it was, it seemed so much like Rome that they actually called them "Little Romes."

The Garden of Eden was a colony of Heaven on earth. The Garden was the beginning of His plan of expansion. From the garden, the colony of the Kingdom of Heaven (the place where it was like Heaven on earth), human beings were supposed to expand and fill the earth.

Kingdom Invasion

God has always intended to invade the earth. God has invasion on his mind. Sounds like a movie, doesn't it? The best movie you've ever seen or heard of. You are a part of this movie. God has intended to fill the earth with the Kingdom of Heaven from the very beginning.

God intends to invade the earth through us. In fact, Jesus Christ is not going to come again to the earth in a physical Second Coming until we as His body have come to the place of the fullness of the stature of the maturity of Christ in the earth (see Eph. 4:13). As His body on earth, we must be proportionate to Jesus Christ, the Head in Heaven.

This means that before He comes back and we have that twinkling-of-an-eye experience and receive our glorified bodies, first He is going to demonstrate Himself to the world through us, no less than how He did Himself, when He physically walked the earth in His single human body. That is a profound statement but it is fully scriptural. Everything that He did—the presence, the power, the demonstration of the Kingdom on the earth—in His single human body when He walked the earth, He will also do through His corporate body that walks the earth now (see Eph. 4:11-16).

Jesus Christ will not have a corporate body that will do less than His individual body. That is not how God works. God increases. God does not lose ground.

The Ever-Expanding and Increasing Kingdom

Isaiah 9:6 is a prophecy about Jesus coming to the earth. It says, "Unto you a child will be born. Unto you a son will be given. The government will rest upon his shoulders." That speaks of the government of the Kingdom of Heaven, which is the greatest and best government the earth has ever known. The same prophecy says that of the increase of His government there shall never be an end.

This does not mean that Jesus came to earth, brought His Kingdom, demonstrated the government of God— and then took His government out of the Earth when He resurrected and ascended to Heaven. In other words, He does not cease to increase His government and then one day (in the Second Coming) bring it again. No. Of the increase of His government there shall never be an end. So, the kingdom of God was here when Jesus walked the earth, the kingdom is here now, and the kingdom is also coming in greater dimensions as time progresses. Many people put off the Kingdom as something that we will not see until Jesus comes in the Second Coming, but that is not scriptural. The manifestation of the Kingdom will increase as time goes on, but make no mistake, the Kingdom is also now! The Kingdom is "at hand."

Jesus expands His kingdom through His family, His Bride, the Church...not through a religion. Jesus did not come to start a religion. Jesus never had any interest in starting a religion called Christianity. He never even called us Christians. Instead, He came to birth a family in the earth. His disciples were called Kingdom citizens, saints, the royal priesthood of God.

God intended to have a habitation on the earth, and He modeled it for us with Israel and the Tabernacle. He "tabernacled" with His people. To this day, He intends to work through us as His habitation in the earth to fill the earth with His ever-expanding Kingdom.

When Jesus came, He prepared a way. He was crucified and raised from the dead, making it possible for us to be born again. He paid the price for our sin and He birthed a new family in the earth. Jesus is the "last Adam," according to First Corinthians 15:45. Why would Jesus be called the last Adam? Because the first Adam was created as a prototype of a Kingdom citizen who would carry the Kingdom of Heaven into the Earth, someone created from two worlds, someone who could carry the Kingdom of Heaven into the earth and advance the Kingdom throughout the earth. When the first Adam sinned, he did not lose only the heights of glory in relationship with God. Adam lost a Kingdom. That is why, when Jesus came *to seek and to save that which was lost"* (Luke 19:10), He came not just to seek and to save individual people, but He also came to seek and save and restore a Kingdom to the earth. He was on a governmental mission as much as He was a personal redemption salvation mission for us.

The Supernatural Church—a New Breed in the Earth

Up until the time Jesus came, there was only one family tree in the earth, the family tree or the line of Adam, the first Adam. All of humanity born after Adam belonged to Adam's family tree. But Adam had become corrupt as the prototype, so everyone else was born corrupt. All of humanity was separated from God.

Jesus came as the second Adam, or rather the Last Adam, to pay the price for our corruption and sin, to birth a new breed in the earth, a new creation. As Jesus' followers, you and I are new creations. 2 Corinthians 5:17 says, *"Therefore if anyone is in Christ, he is a new creation. The old has passed away; behold the new has come"* (ESV). It's as if your umbilical cord was unplugged from the line of the first Adam and plugged into the line of the last Adam, Jesus. Now there is a brand new family tree operating in the earth, the lineage of the last Adam, Jesus Christ. Anyone who is born again today is no longer of the line of the corrupt race of humanity. You are a new breed, a new creature, a new creation.

Jesus named this body of new creations the "church." He could have invented a new word. But instead Jesus took a word that was common in that time and place, the word *ecclesia* ("church" in English). In brief, it means "a called-out assembly of people," the called-out ones. The church is much more than just an assembly of people, though.

In that day, when the Romans were ruling, the word *ecclesia* referred to groups of everyday Jewish citizens who had been called out by the ruling authorities. This called-out assembly operated as an extension of the Roman government in their area. The Romans conferred governmental authority and jurisdiction upon this group of people. This group of citizens was given the authority to decide on court cases. They were given authority over financial matters and all sorts of things that had nothing to do with religion. In fact, the word *ecclesia* has no religious connotation to it at all. It has nothing to do with a religion, and that includes Christianity. The group of people called the *ecclesia* represented an extension of the Roman government.

So when Jesus birthed this new breed, this new family tree, this new family lineage in the earth, only the second family tree in the earth that has ever existed, He called them His *ecclesia*. Why? He was saying, "I'm going up to be with the Father, but you are the extension of My government in the earth."

The Kingdom Lost in the Garden

The mandate of Genesis 1:28—"Fill the earth, be fruitful, multiply, have dominion"—never ended. In fact, Jesus reinforced it when He said, "Make disciples of nations" (see Matt. 28:19). Somehow, we have changed that to "Make disciples." But He said "Disciple nations."

That is a major call. I fully believe that a greater dimension of the Kingdom will come when Jesus physically comes in the Second Coming. In fact, the fullness of the Kingdom will not come until He does come again. But the Kingdom is here now. Since the time Jesus came to the earth the Kingdom has been here, and it is our job to expand it. We are supposed to take dominion in the form of being salt and light in the earth, which means taking dominion over the works of darkness in your own life and in the lives of the people that you minister to and taking authority in the realm of the Spirit in your region.

When Adam and Eve sinned, it was more than just being kicked out of the Garden and losing that heavy glory that had rested on their life. The mantle of authority over the earth that had been placed on them got shifted off. When Adam and Eve sinned, the invisible realm was in total chaos. A governmental regime change took place. Not knowing what they were doing, Adam and Even handed over their delegated authority to the enemy, and satan took authority over the earth. That is why the Bible calls him *"the god of this world"* (2 Cor. 4:4 ESV). That is why satan had legitimate authority when Jesus was in the wilderness going through His temptation, and satan took Him up on the mountaintops to show Him all the kingdoms, saying, "If You will bow down and worship me I will give these kingdoms to You" (see Matt. 4:8-10). Satan had the authority to do that, because it had been given to him, not by God, but by Adam in the Garden.

Humankind had been given so much authority over the earth, that in order for God to correct the mistake that Adam and Eve made, a perfect sacrifice had to be made, in the form of the Last Adam, the God-Man Jesus Christ.

Kingdom Authority Restored to the New Breed

When Jesus came, He created this new breed of people, the new creation in the earth. He took the keys of death and hell and He took away that mantle of delegated authority from satan and conferred it back onto the new breed of believers. He did not give authority to all of humanity, only to the citizens of His Kingdom. But many believers fail to comprehend what has transpired. Because of our ignorance, satan continues to rule the earth. Just because the mantle of authority is back on us does not mean that we are operating in it.

The Church has got to stand up and take our place of authority in the natural realm by first taking our authority in the realm of the Spirit. Jesus' disciples wanted Him to take authority in the natural realm right away. They thought Jesus was there to physically restore the Kingdom in their region and begin to rule and reign in the natural (Luke 17:20; Luke 19:11; Acts 1:6). They thought that was how conquering nations was supposed to work. But Jesus had no intention of doing that yet. It will happen one day, but for now Jesus is invading the earth with His Kingdom by demonstrating Himself through His people, His church.

Instead, at that time Jesus gained authority in the natural realm by being a servant leader. He went low. He loved people. He demonstrated the Kingdom and it gave Him influence wherever He went. In the same way, we must begin to gain influence and to regain a place of authority in the Spirit realm in a region. As believers in a region come together in unity and begin to shift things in the realm of the Spirit, changes manifest in the natural realm.

Restoration of What Began and Was Lost in the Garden

When Adam and Eve were kicked out of the Garden, they did not lose their relationship with God. They still talked with God. Their family members still talked with God. God still talked to Adam and Eve and their kids. But they lost their colony and their kingdom, and they lost the full manifestation of the glory of God upon them.

This is something like believers being only born again enough to go to Heaven, not accessing the fullness of their inheritance this side of eternity. Even with a redemptive, salvation level of relationship with God, they never see the restoration of the former heavenly glory. When Israel was delivered from Egypt, God intended that same generation to actually enter their Promised Land, in their lifetime. That generation failed to do so. Likewise, many believers never actually live in and experience the fullness of what God has destined for them in their lifetime. There is a restoration of the Glory of God that is meant for God's people on this side of eternity. It is a restoration of the glory that was lost in the Garden.

John G. Lake once said this:

> The miracle realm is Man's natural realm. He is by creation the companion of the miracle working God. Sin dethroned Man from the miracle-working realm, but through grace he is coming into his own. In the beginning, Man's spirit was the dominant force in the world. When he sinned, his mind became dominant. Sin dethroned the spirit and crowned the intellect. But grace is restoring the spirit to its place of dominion. And when Man comes to realize this he will live in the realm of the supernatural without effort. No longer will faith be a struggle but a normal living in the realm of God. The spiritual realm places

Men where communion with God is a normal experience. Miracles are then his native breath.

Supernatural Kingdom Culture in the Church

So many believers get saved only to learn how to live according to a religious church culture. There is a religious, worldly culture that has developed in much of the church today. The church that Jesus is building is not called to live according to religion or the world. The church is called to live a supernatural Kingdom culture and lifestyle that is *"on earth as it is in Heaven."* This does not mean that we should throw out the church or become disillusioned with the church. The church is still God's idea and still Jesus' Bride. What must happen is an awakening in the church that causes the church to live as the supernatural body and bride that she is, and to begin to manifest the Kingdom of God in the earth.

The church is supposed to be the agent that represents the Kingdom in the earth, and its culture originates from God, not from the world. In many ways, the journey of Israel is a model for us. Israel was delivered from an oppressive kingdom just as born-again believers are delivered from a demonic kingdom of darkness when we get saved. Israel was then led into the wilderness and up onto the mountain of God, into the supernatural glory of God, where a new lifestyle and culture was delivered to them.

Moses was taken up on the mountain and God gave tablets of stone to him. Not only did He give him a set of laws, the ten commandments, God also gave him blueprints for a tabernacle: This is how much fabric I want you to use. This is how much wood I want you to use. This is how much gold I want you to use. God gave detailed directions about who was to build the tabernacle, and He gave Moses the instructions for a priesthood. This was something so foreign to them. God told Moses, "I want you to put that tabernacle right in the middle of all the camps. Put the priests in the tabernacle and make sure that the whole lifestyle of the people is wrapped around that tabernacle" (see Exod. 23-33). As Israel changed the way they had previously lived and began to live according to this new culture delivered from the glory, then the glory of God filled their nation and tabernacled with them!

God does not want you to get born again and just sit in a church waiting for Jesus to come (although it is good, right, and godly, that you get involved and commit to a local church). He wants to start taking you up the mountain. He wants to start taking you into the experiences of the glory of God.

In the Book of Haggai, God says to the people, "Aren't you tired of making money just to put your money into bags with holes in it? Aren't you tired of feeding yourself and never feeling full? Aren't you tired of drinking just to keep being thirsty?" (see Hag. 1:5-6). He says, "Center your life on My Kingdom and what I have called you to do, not on your own house." He says, "You have focused on your paneled house, and look at Mine. It is destroyed; it is in ruins. But you have built your nice house and you are making money and it goes right into your bag and it is gone tomorrow. Go up on the mountain, gather yourself some wood…" (see Hag. 1:7-9). Prophetically speaking, God is saying, "Get your resources on the mountain. My presence will be your source of supply. Do not look to the things of the earth."

In the New Testament, Jesus said, "Seek first the Kingdom and Hhis righteousness and all these things you have need of will be added to you" (see Matt. 6:33). It is a new culture, a different culture. When you come down from the mountain, you help to synchronize Heaven and earth.

It is a different lifestyle. When you start focusing on the culture of the Kingdom and seeking first the Kingdom, God promises to open up the treasuries of Heaven for you. He says, "I will open up the dew of the earth again. The oil will flow freely from My house, the honey, the wine, and your vats will be full and overflowing" (see Hag. 1:10-11).

This is not something that today's church is living. They live their culture, and that's it. This is why we are not seeing a massive demonstration of the Kingdom around the world. This is why we need the supernatural.

When you do not have the supernatural, it's as if you have let God invade your spirit, and then you lock Him up, throw away the key, and just do church. You live according to church culture and then you go out to your job and live according to work culture, and no one can tell the difference. Where is the salt? Where is the light? The Bible says you are the salt of the earth and that if your salt loses its taste, then it is worth nothing except to be trampled on (see Matt. 5:13).

You do not want to be trampled on. You need to be soaking in His seasoning. You need to be in the glory of God. You need to learn to live by God's supernatural Kingdom culture, not the cultures of this world.

How Is God Restoring What Was Lost?

In the Garden before the Fall, you could say that Adam was completely inverted from the way we are now. The priorities were different. Adam had a body and he had a soul, but the most prominent thing in his life was his lifestyle of the spirit. After he fell, everything got inverted. All of humanity became people of their flesh, dominated by their souls, with spirits that were corrupt and buried within them.

With the coming of the Last Adam, Jesus, God is awakening and restoring people from the inside out. His desire had always been to have a habitation in the midst of his people. In the Old Testament He called the people of Israel His nation. They were like His embassy on earth (see Exod. 19:3-6). In the New Testament, born-again believers are now His royal priesthood, His holy nation, His earthly tabernacle (see 1 Pet. 2:4-5, 9-10; 1 Cor. 3:16).

When Jesus walked the earth, He was the house of God, and He said so. This really tore the religious people up. I once heard a theologian say that when Jesus said, *"I am the way, the truth, and the life"* (John 14:6), the reason this so enraged the Pharisees and the Sadducees was because Jesus used the Hebrew words for the door to the outer court and the door to the inner court and the veil to the Holy of Holies. Those three entryways were known as "the way, the truth, and the life."

The religious people of His day were still doing their sacrifices, and their whole life revolved around the temple. And here's Jesus saying, "Hey, you know the temple life you've practiced for the past several hundred years? A thousand years? I am now the temple." The Jewish religious leaders thought that was a pretty audacious statement. Jesus said, "I am the temple. I am the tabernacle. I am the way, the truth, and the life." This was a new administration of the glory and kingdom of God.

Jesus ascended to His Father and He gave us His Spirit. Now we are the Tabernacle. Born-again believers are now the habitation of God and the expression of God on the earth. Ephesians 2:19-22 says that we are living stones being built into a habitation of God's presence.

God's Idea of Salvation

God's idea of "complete" salvation is not just that we should be born again so we can get into Heaven when we die. Most believers sitting in churches today would define salvation as being born again and going to Heaven one day. That is not God's idea of salvation, and it never has been. God's idea of complete salvation is that you would become born again and then transformed— spirit, soul, and body—into His image, becoming a living stone within the habitation of God, manifesting the supernatural Kingdom everywhere you go.

Many believers today have only heard enough of the salvation message to be saved enough to go to Heaven, but not saved enough to see and manifest the Kingdom on earth. They are like ones who enter the Kingdom but never begin to inherit and possess the Kingdom now. They are like ones who once fell short of God's glory, have now been restored to God's glory, yet never step into that lifestyle of manifesting His glory again in the earth.

Restoration in all Three Parts

God saved you so that you could be restored, spirit, soul, and body. You must understand that all three parts of human beings were damaged at the Fall. The spirit became lifeless and deadened to God. The soul was corrupted. *"The Lord saw that the wickedness of man was great in the earth and that every intention of the thoughts of his heart was only evil continually"* (Gen. 6:5 ESV). And of course, sin and death began to operate in Adam's body and in the earth at large.

It is interesting to note that the condition of the earth mirrors the condition of the people of God. When Adam and Eve were operating in their true call, as a son and daughter of God, the earth was blessed. When they sinned, the earth followed suit. The earth became cursed. This is why Romans chapter 8 says that the earth itself is groaning for the sons of God to be revealed. Why? The earth itself remembers what it was like before Adam and Eve sinned. The earth itself is groaning to be restored. When the New Heaven and the New Earth are formed, I believe that the way the earth functions, the oceans, the land, the temperature, is going to change dramatically. It is going to be restored to the way it was before the Fall.

There are two realities to God's idea of "complete salvation": the judicial reality, which is a work Jesus accomplished "for us," and the organic reality, which is a work Jesus accomplishes "in us." After God establishes a right relation with us, He changes us into His image. This should redefine salvation for us. Judicially, we are received into the state of grace. Organically we associate with the life of God; we learn to live supernatural lives and we actually interact with God. The goal of God's complete salvation is not just forgiveness, but also holiness—that we would become partakers of the divine nature and thus have our whole being permeated with God Hhimself. What is God doing? He is preparing His habitation.

Judicial salvation is like being delivered from Egypt. When Israel was delivered from Egypt, that was like being born again. They were delivered from the bondage of another kingdom. When you are born again, the Bible says that you are pulled out of the kingdom of darkness and put into the Kingdom of His Son (see Col. 1:13). However, being delivered from Egypt, or the kingdom of darkness, is not the fullness of salvation. An entire generation of Israelites died in the wilderness because they did not understand the fullness of what God wanted to do with them. God did not want to just pull them out of Egypt. He wanted to do a whole lot more than that. He wanted that same generation that was pulled out of Egypt to also enter into the Promised Land. He took them into the wilderness, and He put them into martial array. One of the first things that He taught Israel when He pulled them out of Egypt was how to be an army.

Notice how this parallels the Body of Christ. The Body of Christ is referred to as a bride, a house, a gateway—and an army. The name "Lord of Hosts" is used far more than any other name for God in the Bible. That term means "the Lord of Armies." And it means more than angelic armies. We are in His army.

Judicial salvation delivers us from the condemnation of God's wrath. In place of judgment, we have been redeemed, justified, forgiven, reconciled to God through Jesus Christ's shedding of blood, death, and resurrection. Judicial salvation is an outward salvation that qualifies and positions believers to receive and eat of the divine nature of Jesus and thereby be transformed so they can manifest God's glory on the earth.

So we see that the judicial side of salvation qualifies and positions believers for the organic side of salvation where God actually invades you; a physical transaction takes place. It is not just aligning with a Christian creed. A transaction takes place. The seed of God comes into your spirit man. Just as you were born of your parents, you are now born of God. Now you are lifted from the level of natural birth into a place of heavenly birth where your primary citizenship is now in the Kingdom of Heaven.

Organic salvation goes beyond judicial salvation. The judicial side of salvation happens in one single moment, but the organic side of salvation requires a lifestyle of living for the Lord. We are called to live the priestly lifestyle of partaking of the divine nature of Jesus.

"His divine power has granted to us all things that pertain to life and godliness, through the knowledge of him who called

us to his own glory and excellence or virtue. By which he has granted to us his precious and very great promises. So that through them you may become partakers of the divine nature" (2 Peter 1:3-4 ESV). Being delivered from Egypt is one thing. Organic salvation is more like getting Egypt out of us.

On Passover, the sprinkling of the blood on the doorpost was like the judicial salvation. It caused the spirit of death to pass by. But eating the lamb shows organic salvation. Jesus said, *"I am the Bread of Life that came down from heaven. If anyone eats of this bread, he will live forever"* (John 6:51 ESV).

What most believers call salvation is really only the first step in God's idea of complete salvation, the regeneration of the spirit part. Even though most believers stop there, they do not understand even that one point. It is a lot more than saying a prayer and asking Jesus to be the Savior and Lord of your life. Regeneration is when the seed of God comes into your spirit and mingles with it. Your spirit does not become just a container for the Holy Spirit when you are born again. No, the Holy Spirit comes into your spirit and changes your primary nature from its very core (see 1 Cor. 6:17; 2 Cor. 5:17). This is as real as when the Holy Spirit overshadowed Mary and heavenly chromosomes came into Mary's womb and mingled with her chromosomes and created the Christ child. The Father reconnects with your spirit. He disconnects you from the line of the first Adam, and you are born into the line of the last Adam. Just as apples bring forth apples, and oranges bring forth oranges, and your parents brought you forth, now you have been born of God.

Now the Kingdom belongs to you. Not because you have performed well enough to operate in it. The Kingdom belongs to you because your father by blood is the ruler of the Kingdom and you are the heir. Jesus was the first-born among many brethren. You are part of His family. It does not mean you are God or a part of the Trinity, but you are a part of His Family, and it doesn't get any closer than that.

The Bible says that the Kingdom of Heaven is like a mustard seed. The full potential of that tree is in that seed. Everything that will one day be a big tree is in that seed. All that seed needs is sunlight, water, and nourishment. In the same way, if you begin to nurture the seed within your spirit, learning to live in the spirit, in deep relationship and intimacy with God, the life of God in your spirit will begin to saturate your soul. You will fall more and more in love with God and you will start to turn your emotions over to Him. You will become a voluntary lover, not a robot. This begins the next process in God's complete salvation, which is the transformation of the soul.

God is looking for a people who will allow their souls to be transformed. He is looking for a people who will press into Him and catch such a glimpse of Him that they will be undone, ruined forever, so unsatisfied with anything else that they know they must continue this journey with God and be consumed by Him!

Chapter 4

Stillness and Soaking

To launch this book called *School of the Supernatural*, we started out discussing authentic Christianity, and what an authentic supernatural Kingdom life looks like. To make sure that we were all on the same page, I described how we were created as spirit, soul, and body to represent two different worlds so that we could live on the earth and bring the Kingdom of Heaven here. I wanted to be sure you understood what your spirit is for, what your soul is for, and what your body is for. I also wanted you to understand that without living in the supernatural, we cannot advance passed the initial level of salvation; that when you are born again, you are regenerated in spirit. The Holy Spirit comes in you; you have Christ in you, the hope of glory (see Col. 1:27). But that is only the beginning of a much larger process of full salvation, and the rest of the salvation process requires an ongoing encounter with a supernatural God. As we encounter Him daily and deeply, our lives begin to truly become a true habitation or dwelling place for His Spirit, and together with other believers who are living the same way, we are able to manifest His supernatural Kingdom glory to the world.

One of the things that I have learned about God is that He does not always talk to us on our level. God has a language, He has a way that He talks, He has a way that He operates; that is why Moses had to cry out to God and ask God, "God, show me Your ways" (see Exod. 33:13). He wanted to know more about God, because God's ways are not our ways (see Isa. 55:8).

Show Me Your Ways

In this chapter, I want to begin to talk now about some of the mechanics of how to posture yourself to begin to enter into the flow of God's Spirit. God has called us to live in heavenly places in the dimension of the spirit. We are called to be multi-dimensional people. Many people do not understand how to posture themselves before God and get into a position of receiving from Him.

Jesus said, *"Do not labor for the food that leads to nothing, but do labor for the food that leads to eternal life"* (John 6:27). Part of the laboring that you will go through as you begin to live a supernatural lifestyle with God is learning how to posture yourself before Him. The devil will do everything he can to prevent you from rearranging your lifestyle and learning how to get better connected with God. He will do everything he can to distract you, to cut your connection, and to keep you away from that intimate place with God. We need to learn how to press past the enemy and our own deficiencies. We need to persistently echo Moses' request, "Show me Your ways."

In this chapter, I want to share with you the foundation for how I enter into relationship and encounters and into the spirit realm with God. This is the basis for how I have learned to move in miracles, how I have learned to prophesy. These are the things that I still do today to get the revelation that I get.

People say, "You know, where does all this revelation flow from?" Obviously, I study the Word and I read other people's books. But the practical basis for receiving the revelation that comes from God is more than intellectual study. I have learned how to put myself in that place where the river is always flowing and God is always pouring something out. That is what I want to share with you.

Something of the Kingdom is always flowing. God does not sleep. There is a river that is always flowing. He is always there, ready to pour out Hhis Kingdom for us, and we need to be ready and receptive.

The Kingdom Within

Too many people expect God only to do something externally. When people approach God in worship they are looking up to God, they are looking for Him to pour something out from Heaven, and He does that; He fills the atmosphere of our praises.

But the Bible says that the kingdom of Heaven is within you. Luke 17:21 says, *"for indeed the kingdom of God is within you."* Proverbs 20:27 says, *"the spirit of a man is the lamp of the Lord."* As a born-again believer, with Christ in you, your access to the Kingdom of Heaven and into God's spirit realm does not come from God pouring something out on you. You gain access to the Kingdom by learning how to quiet your noisy soul so that, with your spirit, you can hear the still, small voice of His Spirit.

What is the Kingdom? Jesus taught His disciples to pray, *"Your kingdom come, Your will be done on earth as it is in heaven"* (Matt. 6:10 ESV). So one of the easiest ways to describe the kingdom of God is just to say, "as it is in Heaven." Heaven is a perfect picture of what the kingdom of God looks like. The Kingdom of God is a domain, the domain of the King. It is the King's sphere of influence; His will, His purposes, His desires, and the intents of His heart are fulfilled in His domain. God wants His Kingdom to come here so that it can look here on earth as it does in Heaven.

The manifestation of the Kingdom also looks like casting out demons: "If the spirit of God has come upon you to cast out demons, you have seen the kingdom of God come upon you" (see Matt. 12:28). When God's intent is fulfilled on earth as it is in Heaven by, for example, casting a demon out of someone, you have seen the Kingdom come upon them because that is what happens in God's domain, in the King's domain. Other evidences of the Kingdom of God include *"righteousness, peace, and joy in the Holy Spirit"* (Rom. 14:17 ESV). The Kingdom looks like *"as it is in heaven."*

Matthew 10:7 says, "as you go, tell people the kingdom of Heaven is at hand." What does that mean, "at hand"? It means that the kingdom of Heaven is here; it is at hand. And Jesus then basically said to them, "Demonstrate it by healing the sick, raising the dead, cleansing the lepers, and casting out demons."

So the Kingdom is "as it is in Heaven" and the Kingdom is within you. Someplace within you, the kingdom resides "as it is in Heaven." Jesus Christ is the gateway of Heaven. He said "you will see the heavens open, you will see angels of God ascending and descending upon the son of Man" (see John 1:51). This is similar to the angels ascending and descending on the ladder extended from Heaven in Jacob's dream in Genesis 28. Jacob called that place the house of God and the gateway of Heaven. Jesus is now within us. We have now become the house of God, the tabernacle.

That place that God has invaded within your spirit flows with a river of the Spirit. You can access heavenly places there. Not only are you seated with Christ in heavenly places, but He is also Christ in you, the hope of glory (see Eph. 2:6; Col. 1:27). Jesus has become your connection point to the spirit realm in His Kingdom. Your human spirit is now your access point to enter into the things of the Kingdom.

Turn Inward

Kingdom life is about living from the inside out. As Kingdom believers, we are not supposed to live affected by everything around us. We are supposed to live in the Kingdom within us and release that from us and be agents of change in the atmosphere around us. You can have hell and chaos and everything going on around you, but within you is a place like the eye of a hurricane. Within you is the holy of holies where at any given moment that Kingdom river is flowing. You can tap into that place.

God is not as inaccessible as we think He is. It is not as hard to get to God as many believers think it is. God is no longer way out there, even when we are full of doubt, fear, anxiety, and worry. The amazing revelation of the new covenant is that God is now right inside you; therefore you and I have, living within us right now, the greatest source of peace, the greatest government, and the greatest revival to ever touch the earth.

When a body gets a poison in it, the body needs an antidote. The world is crying out for an antidote to its problems. Some people are looking to governments and government administrations to fix things. Some people are crying out to their god, whoever their god may be. Meanwhile, our God is responding back to us and He is saying, "You are the antidote." The greatest antidote that has ever come to earth is living within you. If we can learn to access that place and learn to live out of that place of the spirit, we can turn the world upside down.

You access the realm of God's Spirit by opening the door and turning inward. When you turn to the Lord, the veil is removed (see 2 Cor. 3:16). He is not up there; primarily, He is in your spirit. When you turn to the Lord, a veil is removed, whereupon you begin to see into the supernatural realm. After you learn how to position yourself, then you will get into what you can experience once you position yourself.

Scripture says, "Behold Jesus stands at the door and knocks waiting for us to come and open the door so He can come in and dine with us" (see Rev. 3:20). If you are a born-again believer, Jesus is not outside of you knocking. He is inside, in your spirit, knocking on the door of your soul, your mind, your will, and your emotions. He is saying, "Open up and let's commune together." He is right inside.

Once I picked up one of those snow globes. Within that globe was a whole city, a whole little world of its own. In somewhat the same way, the Kingdom of God is within you. Inside you there is an access point to a whole other world. Entering into God's spirit realm is not asking God to take you up and away; but rather, it is entering into a place of stillness in your spirit. There, you will begin to sense the moving of God's river that is always flowing in you already.

You probably know what that feels like. Maybe you have come in to a worship service kind of dry. You are just not feeling much. Then in the middle of worship, all of a sudden, as you quiet your mind and emotions, you pop into something. You begin to feel the prophetic flow or you begin to feel the presence of God stirring. You have begun to not only feel the presence of God in the room [because He fills our praises and He is enthroned upon our praises (see Ps. 22:3)], but you have also begun to tap into that place within you where the Kingdom is flowing.

When I begin to have encounters with God and receive manifestations of His Kingdom such as words of knowledge or prophecies, it is as simple as, "I am out,"

"I am in." Even while I am writing this, I am moving in between operating on my common sense, using my brain, thinking, and looking up Scriptures; and tuning into my spirit, tapping into revelation, and being sensitive to the Holy Spirit leading me in other directions.

To be supernatural is more natural than we think. We have mystified the supernatural too much. People share supernatural encounters from the pulpit, and I know that they intend for people to be encouraged and to know about what is available in God, but many times when you hear them, it leaves you feeling like it is far beyond your reach. Instead of encouraging you to make you feel as if you can touch that too, it makes you feel the opposite, like such a thing is way out of your league.

These high level things of the supernatural are not as grandiose and mystical as you think they are. Jesus operated this way. Jesus was a normal guy. Granted, He was and is the Son of God, but He put Himself in human form. He was a servant. He could relate to people. He wasn't flaky. Sinners wanted to be around Jesus. They were spellbound by what He said, and it was because He would speak spirit and life through His words. He spoke with great authority. He had compassion on the people. He touched the people and healed them. He got all that from communing with His Father, and so can we.

Pushing Past Distraction

How do we begin to do this? Psalm 46:10 says, *"Be still, and know that I am God."* Isaiah 64:4 says, *"From of old no one has heard or perceived by the ear, no eye has seen a*

God besides you, who acts for those who wait for him" (ESV).
First Samuel 3 illustrates God being found in stillness:

> *Now the young man, Samuel, was ministering to*
> *the Lord under Eli and the word of the Lord was*
> *rare in those days; there no frequent vision. At*
> *that time Eli, whose eyesight had begun to grow*
> *dim so that he could not see, was lying down in*
> *his own place....Samuel was lying down in the*
> *temple of the Lord where the ark of God was*
> (1 Samuel 3:1-2 ESV).

He was resting where the ark (the place of God's presence) was. He was not striving for anything.

> *Then the Lord called Samuel, and he said, 'Here I*
> *am!' and ran to Eli and said, 'Here I am, for you*
> *called me.' But he said, 'I did not call; lie down*
> *again.' So he went and lay down. And the Lord*
> *called again, 'Samuel!' and Samuel arose and went*
> *to Eli and said, 'Here I am, for you called me.' But*
> *he said, 'I did not call, my son; lie down again.'*
> *Now Samuel did not yet know the Lord, and the*
> *word of the Lord had not yet been revealed to him.*
> (1 Samuel 3:4-7 ESV).

Samuel did not yet understand how God speaks. He did not know the voice of the Lord well enough to discern who it was.

Now Eli had gotten himself to a place where he was dull as a doorknob. He was supposed to be the prophetic visionary of the day, yet he was allowing his sons to sleep with the women of Israel right at the gates of God's house. This priest was allowing mixture to come in. The lamp was never supposed to go out in the tabernacle, yet he was lax in tending it. Prophetically speaking, his eyes were growing dim. He could barely see anymore, neither through his physical eyes nor his spiritual eyes. He had no vision. So God had to come to a young boy instead.

"Then Eli perceived that the Lord was calling the young man, therefore, Eli said to Samuel, go lie down and if he calls you, you shall say, Speak Lord, for your servant hears" (1 Sam. 3:8-9 ESV). *"So Samuel obeyed, and the Lord came and spoke to him. Samuel said 'Speak, for your servant hears'"* (1 Sam. 3:10).

Samuel became one of the greatest prophets that God ever had. He learned to hear the voice of God in the place of stillness, soaking and resting in the presence of God, not striving but getting away from the distractions around him.

The enemy understands that the Kingdom of God is within you, waiting for you to connect with Him. So your enemy will do everything he can to distract you with things around you. He does not want you to enter into a place of quiet and stillness so that you can begin to feel the moving of God within you. In fact, we live in a time where people so hate silence that they will turn the TV on in their house even when they are not watching it just to have sound going on, or they will turn music on. People must have some sort of sound or something going on to keep themselves occupied. God is within many believers, knock, knock, knocking, saying, "Come away from everything and quiet yourself so that I can begin to speak to you; I want you to begin to find Me and learn to live in Me."

This is much more important than miracles or other signs of God's presence. In fact, miracles are not always a sign of God's approval. Did you know that? I know people who, once they learn how to tap into the anointing and how to function in their gift, might continue to move in miracles, but outside of the ministry setting they have zero relationship with God for prolonged periods of time. They do not turn from Him completely, but being close to God just for the sake of intimacy lapses. They still spend time with God when they have a meeting coming up, in order to "get into the anointing," but they are using God instead of serving Him out of love.

The Lord spoke to me one time: "I don't want people prostituting the Holy Spirit."

I said, "What? Can you elaborate on that for me, God?"

And He replied, "There are people that have learned the four-step model of how to get into the Spirit, get into the anointing and manifest it and release miracles. It's not that they are operating by demons; they are operating in the things of the kingdom. They have learned how to press into that and not give priority to the intimate relationship with Me. They are still operating on the gift that they developed from a past season of intimacy with Me." Prostitution is when you do something or pay something in order to get a quick one-time moment of intimacy but then afterwards there is no relationship. This is what many people do with God, especially leaders. As leaders, we must learn to maintain a priority of intimacy with

God that is not motivated by needing to get the anointing in order to preach in a meeting.

Real relationship is not a moment of prostitution. Real relationship is sacrificing yourself in relationship day after day.

Giving Yourself to Him

Do not make soaking and waiting on the Lord something you do just to get your handout from God, to get that next fix of the presence of God. Waiting on God means giving ourselves to Him. God once asked me, "Ryan, if I asked you to wait an hour and I did not come until the end of that hour, would you wait? If I asked you to wait three hours, would you wait? If I asked you to wait six hours, would you wait?" Sometimes in the waiting God is challenging our desire for Him and our motives behind the desire.

Over the centuries, many Christians have recognized the value of silence and stillness and waiting. Brother Lawrence was one. He was a monk, and in the 1600s he wrote a book called *The Practice of the Presence of God.* He worked in the kitchen of a monastery and he was very busy. Brother Lawrence trained himself, even in the midst of his day-to-day activity, to be busy at work while also tapping into the things of the Spirit. He worked and fellowshipped with God all throughout his day. Every time Brother Lawrence realized he was not focusing on God, he would stop what he was doing for a few seconds and he would say, "Lord, I set my mind and my affections, my heart on you right now. I love You. I worship You.

I praise You." Then he would go back to work. Thirty minutes later, if he realized he wasn't focusing on God, he would do it again. It got to the point where he was working, and all day long within himself he was worshipping God, staying in the place of flow. He would be in the middle of the kitchen working and he was so sensitive to the slightest touch of God. God would suddenly move in him so powerfully that he would begin to weep—a visitation right in the middle of work! He'd have to walk out and leave the kitchen for a moment to compose himself.

When I read about Brother Lawrence, I decided to put this to the test. I was working in a resort for a summer, and I decided I was not going to tell the other employees that I was a Christian. I was just going to practice the presence of God. It was an accounting-type job and I would be in my office working on a Monday morning and the others would come in—these were adults, not teenagers. They would come in bragging about who they had slept with over the weekend or what new drug they had done or how drunk they got or whatever, and they would get close to my office and they would all stop and I could hear them saying, "shh, shh, let's talk about it over here." They did not know I was Christian, and yet they were not comfortable talking about it around me. There was just something there. Then, later in the day when they would start maybe feeling the negative effects of the night before, they would come into my office and just sit there. At first I thought they were going to ask me something or get something out of the filing cabinet. But they would answer, "Oh, I just like, you know, being in your office. Not sure why. I just like being here. Is that all right?" I began to realize that there was an atmosphere that I had begun to carry. They didn't know what to call it but they felt God on me. Sometimes, just like Brother Lawrence, I would be in the middle of counting money, adding up checks, and the presence of God would come all over me so powerfully that I would just about lose it in the office. I had some amazing encounters with God—right in the middle of my workday. God was trying to show me, "I can be a part of your life anywhere you go, at any time; it does not matter what you're doing."

Besides Brother Lawrence, another person who modeled soaking in God's presence was Sadhu Sundar Singh (1889-1929). He had a "Damascus Road" experience and conversion with Jesus like the apostle Paul. Afterward, he continued to dress in the yellow robe and turban he had worn as a Sikh. The yellow robe was the "uniform" of a Hindu sadhu. He was often rejected and persecuted, but he walked from place to place, preaching the Gospel of the Kingdom, performing miracles, exemplifying humility, and lifting up Jesus. His model for accessing God's heavenly realm was the "four R's of contemplation." He would *read* a Scripture from the Bible out loud quickly and listen carefully, just to begin to focus his mind. Then he would begin to *respond* to the Scriptures with his heart and his mind. Next, he would begin to *recollect* himself with meditation, quieting himself and focusing on those Scriptures. Finally, he would begin to *rest* in the presence of God.

A French woman called Madame Jeanne Guyon (1647-1717) also wrote about her spiritual life. The essence of her teaching was that anybody, even people who could barely read, could enter into the presence of God. Madame Guyon learned to do what Sadhu Sundar Singh would do later, and that is, she would begin to read the Scriptures and suddenly a Scripture would pop out at her. She would feel the presence of God on that Scripture and would stop right there. She would continue to meditate on that Word, and the presence of God would strengthen. When the presence of God would wane, she would read some more until she felt the presence of God again. She taught people how to center themselves in quietness and stillness and to learn how to abide in that place. Madame Guyon was Catholic, and the Church authorities of the time considered her heretical, in spite of their own long tradition of contemplative prayer and the prayer model called Lectio Divina.

It may have seemed heretical then, but all it amounts to is "recollecting," letting go of everything but God being present here and now, casting all your anxieties on Him, practicing the presence of God in the room with you at that very moment, using your imagination to picture the cloud of God's presence wrapping around you. This is not far-fetched or New Age or weird. It is a practical way to open up the gateway to the river of the Spirit within.

Many people do not like to get quiet. When they get quiet, the things that they have allowed the enemy to do inside of them come to the surface. That is why people have the TV on all the time or listen to the radio or music. Anything but stillness; anything but quiet.

In the prayer of quiet, we are hushed at the center of our being and we enter a listening stillness. All of the outward and inward distractions have been silenced, and our spirit is completely engaged and on alert to hear and experience God. We bask in the warmth of His presence and simply behold Him. We do not talk. Catholic contemplatives would call this a stage of ecstasy. Peter called it a trance (see Acts 10:10). The Greek word *ectasis is* most often translated as *trance.* This state of being is granted by the Lord Himself and cannot be achieved by our own efforts. It is a state of being completely unaware of our surroundings and just completely caught up with the Lord.

Becoming still remains the greatest challenge. If we are going to commune with God, first we must become still. Habakkuk went to his guard post to pray (see Hab. 2:1). In the early morning when it was still dark, Jesus departed to a lonely place to pray, and after a day's ministry, Jesus went to a mountain to pray (see Luke 9:28). They reduced the outward distractions around them.

But what about inward distractions? Most believers are completely dominated by their minds. They can't stop their minds from working when they want. You must learn to beat your mind into subjection. Your spirit needs to become the master of your mind. One practical tip is this: if you think of things to do, write them down. Then say to your mind, "You can't tell me things to do anymore. All my to-do list is written down, so be quiet." (Obviously, if your sins come to mind, confess them and get rid of them. Then you can't blame that as a distraction anymore, either.) Your mind wants to be in charge. It wants to know what is going on and it wants to understand it, analyze it.

If your mind wanders aimlessly, speak in tongues. Paul said "When I speak in tongues, my mind is unfruitful but my spirit is speaking to the Lord" (see 1 Cor. 14:14). I am not just talking about five minutes. I would speak in tongues for hours until my mind completely gave up and I didn't even know what I was doing anymore. It was great because my mind learned who was boss. Speaking in tongues energizes your spirit. It causes your spirit to open up. It sensitizes your spirit. It is like lifting weights for the body.

Sing and praise and worship God. Focus on Jesus. Meditate on the Word until your mind is still. At first, you will be able to handle this only ten or twenty minutes a day. You have got to persist if you want to establish new habits that will defeat distractions and allow you to enter God's presence.

Life as a Branch

In talking about learning to quiet ourselves before the Lord, the importance of it is so that we can posture ourselves to receive of God's presence, His peace, His *life*. I call this the "Branch Life." A branch does not have to do anything to be successful and to fulfill its purpose other than to abide in the vine. It stays connected to the source of life that flows in and sustains success. In the spontaneous flow of God's Spirit, you will be receptive. Now God can take you places in the Spirit or show you words of knowledge or give you prophetic words. He can send an angel to you. In the place of stillness, God can tell you whatever He wants to speak.

In learning to quiet ourselves and be receptive to God we are looking at five ingredients of a quiet, still, contemplative state: (1) Physical calm, (2) focused attention, (3) letting be, (4) staying connected, and (5) spontaneous flow. When you learn to bring these five ingredients together in posturing yourself before the Lord, then you will find that you are living the "Branch Life" and receiving the very Life of God, partaking of His divine nature (see 2 Pet. 1:4).

You Become What You Behold

Stillness, soaking, posturing, and living the "Branch Life" are also important because you become what you behold. *"But we all, with unveiled face, beholding as in a mirror the glory of the Lord, are being transformed into the same image from glory to glory, just as by the spirit of the Lord"* (2 Cor. 3:18).

The more you behold Him, the more you become like Him. What you think about or meditate on, fuels you. You end up reproducing that in your life.

Our ultimate goal in life should be to be wholeheartedly, passionately in love with God; and out of that relationship, become like Him and display His goodness, power, love, and character to the world around us, everywhere we go!

Now, after learning to posture yourself to receive from God, how does God speak? What do His language and communications sound like? If I'm supposed to experience "on earth as it is in Heaven," then what will that feel like and how will I know when it is happening? All these questions and more will be answered as we move on to the next chapter, *Spirit Talk.*

Chapter 5

Spirit Talk

God has created a form of communication for the Spirit realm. He uses this form of communication and so does the devil. After all, satan was created by God as a spiritual being and was once a very high-powered angel in Heaven, until he rebelled against God. Satan understands and speaks the language of the spirit realm that God created. Each of us needs to learn the basics of how God speaks and what the language of the Spirit world sounds like. Why is that important? Because you need to not only understand how to hear God, but you also need to be able to discern when you're hearing from the enemy. Our failure to understand the ways of the Spirit world means that the Church has been taken advantage of, unnecessarily, by satan. We need to understand the Spirit world and the language of it. Our lack of understanding concerning the spirit realm that God created has caused many in the church to fear anything "too spiritual" or "too experiential." In fact, many in the church have given spirit realm activity completely over to the devil by naming it "New Age" or "demonic." God created the spirit realm, or unseen realm, and He created

His people to interact with Him in it. The devil is a liar and a deceiver and only tries to deceive God's people by counterfeiting the supernatural and discrediting the supernatural in the eyes of God's people.

The lifestyle of a believer must include a supernatural hearing of the words that God speaks. This is reflected in Scripture. In John 6:63, Jesus says: *"It is the Spirit who gives life. The flesh profits nothing. The words that I speak to you are spirit and they are life."* And in Matthew 4:4, Jesus says, *"It is written, Man shall not live by bread alone, but by every word that proceeds from the mouth of God."*

The voice of God is our life and our light. Throughout the Bible God makes one point very clear. He says, "If you will obey My voice, that will decide whether you live a life of life or death, blessing or cursing." I highly encourage you to read more of this passage in Deuteronomy 30:11-20, because it tells us just how vitally important it is to not just have a head knowledge of God but to actually live a life of intimate relationship with Him, hearing Him and obeying Him every step we take.

You need to be able to hear the voice of God in order to obey it. It is possible for a born-again believer to live a life under the effects of the curse we've already been delivered from, more than the healthy and blessed life that God intends for us.

Staying Connected

Just because you are a born-again believer does not guarantee that you will go through the rest of your life being successful and blessed and having the presence of God in your life. There are conditions. And one of those is that you stay connected to the vine (see John 15). In this passage, Jesus tells us that the fruit we bear in our lives is directly related to where or who we are "abiding" in. Yes, positionally, we are "in Christ" as born-again believers. However, are you experiencing a daily lifestyle of "abiding in Him," in intimate relationship with Him?

Let's relate this to marriage. You can be married by fact of ceremony and union, but that does not necessarily mean you are "experiencing" the effects of intimacy and union with your spouse. It doesn't guarantee that the fruit of love and intimacy is manifesting in your relationship with your spouse. It is the same in your relationship with God. You can be a born-again believer, a new creation, because of the moment you prayed a prayer from your heart and were born-again. However, it is possible to go on living outside of the fruit, happiness, and blessing that God intends for you in your relationship with Him. This is where many believers live today: born-again, but living under the effects of the world and the curse that they've already been delivered from by Jesus' loving sacrifice on the cross!

Real, daily, intimate relationship with God is your very source of life! Jesus said, *"The words that I speak to you are spirit, and they are life"* (John 6:63). When you hear the voice of God, it is like food to your Spirit. We feed our bodies. We drink. We eat. We feed our minds. Our minds are working and active. But oftentimes our spirits are neglected. For most of us, our spirits are lethargic and apathetic instead of being active and flowing in the things of the Kingdom. A good part of the reason is that people are not hearing the voice of God on a regular basis.

Every single person should be able to hear God's voice. He is our Bridegroom. How many brides and bridegrooms do you know who don't talk daily? How many people in an intense love relationship do not talk daily or at least every other day?

God has something to say and our source of life is the voice of God. We start to become religious people, which is not necessarily a good thing, as soon as we start just doing our church thing and pride ourselves in the fact that we "know our Bible." Jesus said, *"You search the Scriptures because in them you think you have eternal life. But these Scriptures are to lead you to Me. The living Word that you might have life"* (John 5:39-40). Oh, there is inherent power in the written and confessed Word of God. But you are supposed to have the living, spoken, "now" word, too.

If you are not living a lifestyle of actually hearing the voice of God, then your relationship is growing dim and your life source is growing dim and your spirit is not being fed. In the same way, if you go too long without eating, your body gets weaker and weaker. We must begin putting as much focus on our spiritual life as we do on the other areas of our life.

Every believer has to take personal responsibility for his or her relationship with God. To hear a message on Sunday morning or Wednesday night or to rely on the ministry at a church to be our only source of spiritual food and substance is not legitimate, authentic Christianity.

That is meeting-based Christianity. How do believers live the other 166 hours of the week outside of those two or three hours on Sunday morning? How would it change our world if millions of believers began to take personal responsibility for their spiritual lives?

How many people come to church Sunday after Sunday and have not been in communication with God all week long? They show up on Sunday out of commitment, and their spirits are so lethargic that they hardly want to be there. "Feed me, feed me!" they say. They rely on the worship leader to create atmosphere. If there is not breakthrough, it is the worship leader's fault. If the preaching is not good, it is because the pastor didn't pray enough or didn't study enough. Could it actually be partly due to the fact that the worship leader and pastor have to work so hard to break through the hard, oppressive atmosphere that was brought into the building by so many people that are carrying the weight of the world, because they've been disconnected from God all week?

What happens when people *have* been communicating with God all week and they come on Sunday morning *not* needing life from others but having life to give? What happens when thousands of people come to our corporate church meetings, already "filled up," with a testimony about how God has been rocking their world during the week? That would create a momentum of the Kingdom that could not be stopped.

We must get into a mindset in the body of Christ of advancing and building and momentum, not just maintaining. Just because massive numbers are in a church doesn't mean there is massive impact that's taking place in a region. You can have a church that is a mile wide and only an inch deep. We need quantity, but we must also have quality—depth of supernatural relationship with God. And when people are not connected to their life source of God's voice and His presence all throughout their week, then Sunday mornings are like trying to raise the dead before they can actually be fed.

Adam and Eve knew the sound of the Lord God in the Garden. Most believers today do not even hear the sound of the Lord when He comes into their garden. God is still waiting in our garden for us to return to intimate, daily relationship again.

Logos and Rhema

Before I go any further on the subject of "Spirit Talk," I need to explain two different vehicles that God uses to speak His words to you and how they relate to your life today. There are two Greek words for "word" in the New Testament: *logos* and *rhema. Logos* simply means the written word, the Bible. The word *rhema* means the spoken word. So a *logos* is something that has already been written down, by inspiration of the Holy Spirit, at a time in the past (the Bible); and *rhema* is something that is being spoken in the now. *Rhema* is always fresh. It is spoken directly from the Lord.

Here is a passage in which Jesus used both words. Jesus is speaking to His Father: *"I have manifested Your name to the people whom You gave Me out of the world. Yours they were and You gave them to Me, and they have kept Your word"* (John 17:6 ESV). That "word" is *logos*. The people had kept the Father's written word in the form of the Bible they had during that time: the Torah. He goes on to say, *"Now they know that everything that You have given Me is from You. For I have given them the **words** that You gave Me..."* (John 17:7-8 ESV). That time, "words" is *rhema*. So He is saying, "I gave them Your written word and they obeyed it, but I also gave them the words that You gave Me for them, the spoken revelatory word from Heaven. And they have received them and have come to know in truth that I came from You and they have believed that You sent Me."

The mixture of the two, both the *logos* word and the revelatory *rhema* word, is what caused the people to believe that He was truly sent from God. The world is not going to believe that we are truly God's people on the earth and have the glory of God on our lives just because we have the Bible. As incredible and as Holy Spirit inspired as the Bible is, it is just a book to the people of the world until we deliver God's written Word to them under a fresh anointing of God's Spirit for their lives today. There has to be life to it, a "now" word for this season. A weary world is looking for something more than just another religious book.

Law vs. Relationship

The difference between the spirit of religion and an intimate, lively, active, supernatural relationship with God is the difference between *logos* and *rhema*. The spirit of religion will get you to worship a Book and its rules.

Religion consists of the human rules and cultural ways of approaching a god. Wherever the religious spirit is strong, you will notice a lack of the prophetic *rhema* word of God. The *rhema* word of God is the only thing that combats and tears down the religious spirit. The religious spirit is stale. The prophetic, revelatory *rhema* word of God is fresh. It is like the manna that showed up on the ground every morning for the Israelites.

You can be a prophetic person, but if you start disconnecting from hearing the voice of the Spirit of God for a period of time, you are going to start getting crusty and religious. Religion worships the written word only, and is in bondage to the law. Relationship, however, is a healthy mixture of the *logos* and the *rhema*. We must maintain a healthy balance in our lives of the written word of God and the spoken "now" words and activity of God. People who love the power of God often criticize those who seem to them to only acknowledge the written word of God. People who have a love and knowledge of the written word of God, the Bible, often criticize those who operate in the power of God, calling them flaky, unstable, off-balance scripturally and either deceived or in error. There must be a balance! In Matthew 22:29, Jesus said, *"You are wrong* [other versions say *deceived* or *in error*], *because you know neither the Scriptures nor the power of God"* (ESV).

Because of a fear of the supernatural, a fear of being deceived, and a fear of being "in error," many believers have disdained the experiential, supernatural side of authentic Christianity and embraced a purely mental or emotional Christianity. They label the more experiential side of Christianity as occult-like, new-age like, and even to be feared as deceptive. Ironically, as Jesus states above, it is possible to have an incredibly rich and deep knowledge of the Scriptures and actually be completely deceived and even in error if you do not also have an "experiential" knowledge of God and His supernatural power in your life!

Sometimes the most charismatic, prophetic, apostolic people are the ones who have lost their love for the written Word of God. Because they are so eager to hear the next prophetic word, the next big thing, they have lost their love for the simple revelations in the Word of God. We need to love the Word of God. The Bible is a portal. It is a doorway into the very glory of God. But only if God breathes on it. If God does not breathe on it, it is just a book. But as soon as God breathes on it, this book suddenly becomes a doorway from the written word into the living Word. That is what makes this Book supernatural.

I must emphasize how important a love for the Bible is to all Christians. To be ready to hear the fresh *rhema* word from God, you have to fill yourself with the written *logos* of God, whether you feel like it or not. The Bible is our foundation for all relationship with God. It is the fuel that God can ignite. When God's fire comes upon your life, what is going to keep it burning? What kind of fuel have you put into yourself? Do you want to be just a shooting star, flash-in-the pan kind of person, or do you want to be a consistently living, breathing habitation of God like Jesus? Jesus was and is the manifestation of the

Word. Jesus was and is perfect theology. Jesus *was* and *is* the Word (see John 1:14-18).

This love for the Word of God is what has given me such a great foundation in my life. My love and honor for the Word of God is what has become the launch pad for my intimate relationship with God. I have learned that if I fill myself with the Bible, God uses it as a foundation and a launch pad into greater experience and revelation of Him. After I have filled myself with the *logos* Word of God, then all of a sudden when I least expect it, the breath of God will come. God will breathe on Scriptures that I have just been meditating on, and I will get hours and hours of revelation in a moment. I will have to pull off to the side of the road and write it down as fast as I can or record it on my iPhone. But that would not happen if I did not give God something to breathe on.

What you fill yourself with either becomes fuel for God or fuel for the enemy. If you are a Kingdom citizen, there is no neutral ground. You are either filling yourself with something that will benefit your relationship with God, or you are filling yourself with something that is going to benefit the advancement of the kingdom of darkness in your life. This does not necessarily mean that you're worshiping Satan or watching pornography or doing overt evil. It could be that you are just filling your time with nonsense.

Another way to discern whether or not you're using your time well is to think about "first fruits." First fruits does not just mean the giving of your tithe or financial offering; first fruits indicate what you value most in your life. What do you give your time to? What do you love? What do you think about? Take every area—your time, your money, your thoughts, your emotions, your relationships—and ask yourself in every one of those areas, "Do I consider God first? Am I giving Him the first fruits in every single one of those areas?" That is a convicting question. But the Bible says, "Seek first the Kingdom and His righteousness and all these things that you have need of will be added to you" (see Matt. 6:33).

The Language of the Spirit

Now let's get into the actual mechanics of hearing the voice of God. How does the spirit world communicate? What is the language of the Spirit?

"The natural person does not accept the things of the Spirit of God, for they are folly to him, and he is not able to understand them because they are spiritually discerned" (1 Cor. 2:14 ESV). God's ways are higher than our ways. His thoughts are higher than our thoughts (see Isa. 55:8-9).

We seem to expect God to speak to us in a way that we are accustomed to. God does not work that way. God has a language and a way of speaking, and we have to adapt to the way He speaks. So what does the voice of the Spirit sound like? What I'm about to share with you sounds so simple and is by no means meant to limit how God can speak to you, but what I'm about to share with you will give you the right foundation for how God speaks, how the devil speaks and how any spirit realm (unseen realm) communication will come to you.

Spirit realm communication comes as a spontaneous thought, a spontaneous idea, a spontaneous word, a spontaneous feeling, an impression, or even a spontaneous vision.

Communication from the spirit realm, whether it be from God or from satan, comes spontaneously in one of the ways listed above.

The Hebrew word *naba* means "prophet" or "to prophesy." Whenever you see a prophet in the Old Testament, the word *naba* is used. The word *naba* also means "to bubble up." When prophets prophesy, they will quiet themselves and then tune in to the spontaneous bubbling up of thoughts coming to them. This is why it is so important to learn how to posture yourself and focus on the Lord, in order to focus on your spirit, which is where God's Spirit communicates with you.

When you quiet yourself, your spiritual senses quicken. You begin to discern the moving of the Holy Spirit within you. You may begin to realize that angels are in the room. Scriptures will come alive. Thoughts and ideas will come to your mind. Visions will often come to my mind. You may get words of knowledge; pictures often come to my mind spontaneously. You may see highlights on different parts of people's bodies to show you that there is something wrong with this bone or that area or the kidneys or whatever; this is often how I get words of knowledge for healing. You may get prophetic words for people. It comes very gently. It may seem like a faint whisper because you are not used to hearing it. You could miss it if you do not pay attention.

So in the beginning, you have got to start to cultivate the ability to discern spiritual communication.

Whose Voice?

When the Holy Spirit speaks to you, He will speak to you in your spirit. But *His communication is registered in your mind.* That is the way God created us. He will speak to you spontaneously and directly into your spirit, but you process that communication with your mind.

The enemy, satan, does not speak to you through your spirit. Demons speak directly to your mind by inserting thoughts into your mind. It is important to understand the difference. They can do that. Not every thought that you think is yours. Your mind is a platform and a processor for more than just your thoughts. Your mind is a processor for spirit world communications as well.

So your mind becomes the place of victory or defeat. Your victory is won when you recognize a thought for what it is, and then choose whether to accept it or not.

> *For the weapons of our warfare are not of the flesh but have divine power to destroy strongholds. We destroy arguments and every lofty opinion raised against the knowledge of God and take every* **thought** *captive to obey Christ. Being ready to punish every disobedience when your obedience is complete* (2 Corinthians 10:4-6 ESV).

In other words, our spiritual warfare is not carnal. We do not wage warfare according to the flesh. But the weapons of our warfare have divine power to destroy strongholds, arguments, and every lofty opinion raised against God.

The problem is that because many people do not understand what spirit world communication sounds like or feels like, they can't discern when it is God who is speaking to them. This is a point of big confusion for people. They wonder, "Is this me? Is this God? Is this the enemy?" The only way to become mature is to begin to train yourself in hearing the voice of God. Test things out in your life. See if they line up with the character of the Word. We live in a society that is very different from Bible times. So God will speak some things to you that are not literally word for word in the Bible. We need to look to see if what we are hearing lines up with the *character* of the Word.

Look to see how the word makes you feel. When God speaks to you, He will not come and bring condemnation to you. There is a difference between condemnation and conviction. Conviction is a gift from the Holy Spirit and something we should ask God for, lest we grieve the Holy Spirit. Condemnation and guilt and shame show you that the enemy is speaking to you, because they line up with his character. Discernment is a learning process.

In the spirit realm, speaking with your mouth and with actual words is completely unnecessary. In the spirit realm, it is actually a lower form of communication. In the spirit realm, you communicate with instant communication, spirit to spirit, thought to thought. I have had hour-long communications with the Lord in visionary form where we have never opened our mouths but we said a whole lot. Communication was taking place.

People can become too afraid to listen for God's voice in their spirit, even though God created us to communicate with Him in this way. They think they will be deceived. It's as if they have more faith in the enemy to deceive than they do in God to protect them. Fear, as you know, is actually a form of faith in the enemy. When you have fear of something, aren't you putting your faith in something the devil can do in your life? Do not "throw the baby out with the bath water" just because of fear of deception.

Now, before we move on in this subject, I want to remind you of this:

> **Spirit realm communication comes as a spontaneous thought, a spontaneous idea, a spontaneous word, a spontaneous feeling, an impression, or even a spontaneous vision.**

Right Brain vs. Left Brain

In my journey of learning to hear the voice of God, I made a discovery that was new to me but not new to the scientific world. My understanding that the spirit realm communicates *spontaneously* really became practical in my daily life as I discovered how the human brain discerns, deciphers, and filters spontaneous information. Most people know that we have different departments in our brains. It is not as exactly divided as first reported in the studies, but it is true that certain parts of your brain do more analytical things; and for the purpose of discussion, we will call these parts the *left brain*. That part of your brain handles things such as speaking, number skills, writing, reading, reasoning, and analytical thoughts. Another part of your brain, which we will call the *right brain,* handles music, three-dimensional forms, and art. It also processes intuition, imagination, and spontaneity. That part of your brain processes spontaneous things. What we can learn from this is that when God speaks to our spirit in His spontaneous way, we need to process it in a spontaneous way. So we must learn to use the spontaneous functions of our brain in order to perceive and process God's communications.

This is why prophetic people are more "right-brained." They tend to be very artsy, very musical. And the people who are the most frustrated in hearing the voice of God are the analytical, left-brained ones. They reason about things all the time. They try to understand everything before they accept it.

Interestingly, in the Kingdom, Jesus never seemed interested in having us understand something before we said, "I believe." He did it the other way around. Believe. Have faith. *Then* understanding comes. We accepted Jesus as our Savior not understanding the fullness of what was going on, and we are still today getting revelation on that.

Do you tend to operate more left-brained or right-brained? You can go online and search for "right brain/left brain tests" and find out. I used to be more left-brained, and I have had to work to develop right-brained activity. As a public speaker, which is a left-brain activity, I have had to work at hearing God. It's not that God was not speaking; I was not perceiving it, or when I did perceive it, immediate questions came to mind and they shut off the flow. My doubts and deliberations shut off the flow of revelation, like hitting "Pause" on the recording. By the time I hit "Play" again, God was done. And I missed it.

I've had to learn to gain mastery over my mind. Because God's voice registers as spontaneous communication, and the right hemisphere of the brain processes spontaneity, we must learn to still and quiet our active left brains in order to tune into spontaneity. How can you loosen up and learn to flow with the spontaneity of the Spirit? Here are some ideas.

In Second Kings 3:14-15, we see that the prophet Elisha used music. He said, *"Bring me a musician."* Why did he ask for a musician? Because music unplugs you from those left-brain activities of reasoning and thinking, and it helps tune you into spontaneity. Worship helps you, as well. When the musician played, the hand of the Lord came upon him and Elisha prophesied.

Many people go out into nature when they pray. They find that nature helps them tune into spontaneity. Art helps you too, looking at it or doing it. Another thing that tunes you into your right brain is speaking in tongues. Even when you do not have music, art, or nature, you can speak in tongues, your private prayer language. Speaking in tongues quiets your mind and activates and sensitizes your spirit. Your spirit is praying (see 1 Cor. 14:14).

I talk with people all the time who are getting major breakthroughs in hearing the voice of God after getting revelation on the difference between right-brain and left-brain people. Left-brain people are always especially thankful because this understanding has helped them to realize that there is nothing wrong with them. They now realize that they are the way they are because God created them that way and it is nothing to be ashamed of. However, they are also realizing that anyone and everyone, even primarily left-brained people, can learn to fully utilize their minds in a way that adapts to the way God speaks. As I mentioned at the beginning of this chapter, God has a way of speaking and He does not bend to our level. He expects us to learn His ways and communicate with Him on that level. Every single one of you can hear the voice of God; and I believe the secrets mentioned above can help a more left-brained person to begin to posture yourself in a way that will literally explode your relationship with God!

Tuning Into Spontaneous Spiritual Vision

When Habakkuk went out to pray, he would *watch* to see what God would say. He used his spiritual eyes. He understood that a large part of the language of the spirit world involved *seeing* with your inner eye, your imagination. This is often where people get nervous because they label this as New Age. God gave you an imagination, a mind's eye, for a reason. Yes, the devil has perverted it and speaks to people in the occult and New Age by these means as well, but that does not do away with spiritual vision for God's people. After all, God created it. I will go into this in more detail in future chapters.

One of the things you will notice about the prophets in the Bible is that they learned to peer into the spirit realm. Anytime they felt the presence of God, the slightest touch of the Lord, they would ignore everyone around them. You need to begin to learn to pay attention to those soft movements, those senses that you could just as easily pass by. Start to recognize those. Focus on those spontaneous thoughts. Focus on those spontaneous ideas. Focus on those spontaneous visions. If you do not give some sort of regard to those slight impressions, God will not give any more. It is like receiving a prophetic word. Oftentimes, God will give you one little nugget. It does not even feel like a full prophetic word. It may be just a Scripture. But God will not give you more of the prophetic word until you are faithful to share that little nugget. In the same way, when God is communicating to you, if you ignore the promptings because you do not know what to look for, then the whole communication will be shut off.

Often, when I begin to tune in to the Spirit, I begin to recognize the flow of the Spirit. The Spirit was flowing all along, but I just now tapped into it. I had to open my spiritual eyes and watch what was going on in the spiritual realm.

Living in the Supernatural = Maintenance

You must learn to sanctify your imagination and your spiritual senses to the Lord. To sanctify means to "set apart." Living a supernatural lifestyle requires setting yourself apart to the Lord and that requires maintenance. Part of this comes as you soak in the presence of God. Psalm 36:9 says, *"For with You is the fountain of life. In Your light we see light."* The Lord showed me in a vision once that if you are shut up in a pitch-black room where it is so dark you can't even see a hand in front of your face, and suddenly the door to the outdoors is opened up and it is a bright, sunny day, you cannot see anything at first. Even in the natural, even though you are now in the light, it takes your natural eyes a moment to adjust so that you can see what is already right in front of you.

In the same way, in the Spirit, you are in the light. You're in the place where you should be able to see, just as you are seated with Christ in heavenly places (see Eph. 2:6). You are seated where you should be able to see. Everything is there, but you can't see. Why? Because you need time to train your senses, for your senses to adjust. You need time for your spiritual eyes to adjust to that bright light of Heaven. Suddenly things begin to come into clarity. By spending time in contemplative prayer, posturing yourself before the Lord, focusing and meditating on the kinds of encounters that people had in the Bible, you are filling your mind with things for God to breathe on. By setting your mind solely on Jesus, worshiping Jesus, worshiping in your car, by doing those kinds of things, you are soaking your spiritual senses in the presence of God. Over time they begin to open up.

So much of living in the supernatural is maintenance. People choose not to pay attention to their spiritual life for a whole month and then a month later get into prayer and expect to have this big visitation of intimacy with Jesus. It

does not work that way. It's not that God is choosing not to
reveal Himself to you; it's simply that you are now desen-
sitized to His presence. For example, if you are a weight-
lifter and you could bench-press three hundred and fifty
pounds and then you took several months off, you would
not be able to lift as much when you went back to the
gym. It requires consistency and maintenance. It requires
dedicating your senses to God, keeping them clean and
pure, and spending time in the presence of God.

*In the realm of the spirit, communication comes as sponta-
neous thoughts, ideas, impressions, words, and visions.* As you
learn how to posture yourself to tap into the right side of
your brain and process the revelation, you will be able to
receive it consistently.

Living in the supernatural and maintaining a relationship with God is about consistently stewarding your
spiritual life. You feed your body every day. You feed
your mind. You feed your soul every day. We must put as
much—or more—emphasis on our spirits. We should build
up our spiritual muscles by seeking after God and worshiping Him. We should feed our spirits, living a lifestyle
that brings us into alignment with God. It is a daily thing.

Some of your greatest encounters and most intimate
moments with God will come when you have just been
faithful with the little things and faithful in taking care of
your spiritual life; and then one day, when God chooses,
He just shows up and surprises you. And guess what?
You will be sensitive enough to perceive it.

In the last couple of chapters, we have learned how
to posture and position ourselves in order to receive

supernaturally from God, and we have also learned how He communicates to us supernaturally, once we've postured ourselves. Now, some of you, after putting the last two chapters into practice, might find that you are struggling in really perceiving and hearing from God in these supernatural ways. Read on in the next chapter as I discuss both what hinders your spiritual senses and what awakens and activates your spiritual senses….

Chapter 6

Activating Your Spiritual Senses

His servant was terrified. Surely they were about to be annihilated. But Elisha, who already knew that everything would turn out well because he saw what was happening in the spirit realm, prayed and said, *"'Lord, I pray, open his eyes that he may see.' Then the Lord opened the eyes of the young man, and he saw. And behold, the mountain was full of horses and chariots of fire all around..."* (2 Kings 6:17).

Elisha was operating with a spiritual sense of sight that his servant was not—until he prayed. This shows us that it is possible to have your spiritual eyes opened and your spiritual senses activated. Not only is it possible to see into the realm of the spirit, but it is also possible, through a prayer of impartation, to get help seeing in the Spirit.

When I talk about activating your spiritual senses, this can be related to your natural senses. In the natural you have five senses. You can see, hear, smell, touch, and taste. Just as your body has these senses, so does your spirit. You can perceive God's realm spiritually by seeing, hearing, smelling, touching, and tasting. This will all be explained in more detail throughout the remainder of this book.

Hebrews 5:14 refers to *"those who by reason of use have their senses exercised to discern both good and evil."* Another version of that passage says that "by reason of consistent practice their senses are exercised to discern both good and evil or to discern the things in the Spirit." Learning to live a supernatural lifestyle requires spiritual senses that are active and functional and this requires coming into alignment with God.

Alignment

If you can keep yourself in alignment with God, then you will operate in the things of the Spirit and your spiritual senses will stay active. If you come out of alignment with God, your spiritual senses begin to cloud over and gradually you will become numb to the things of the Spirit. Like muscles that go unused for a long time, your spiritual senses become atrophied.

When you stay aligned with God, you experience the open door of Heaven in your life. It is like you have used the right combination to open the lock. You have turned the knob until things perfectly aligned, and then they just click into place and you open the door.

But it is not always easy. Like Elisha's servant, we have major hindrances to walking through that open door. And the same things that stopped Israel from entering into the Promised Land are the same kinds of things that stop believers today from operating in the fullness of the Holy Spirit with their spiritual senses fully activated.

In the third chapter of Hebrews, God warns us about some of the things that blocked and hindered the Israelites from taking the Promised Land. Prophetically speaking, the Promised Land for them represents the fullness of the Spirit for us. It represented the fulfillment of promises for them, and it meant that they would be laying hold of their inheritance. When we step into our "Promised Land," we too are operating in our inheritance in this lifetime.

Part of our inheritance is the fruit of the new covenant. Part of the fruit of the new covenant is having a brand-new relationship with God that gives us the ability to coexist with Him, operating in the earthly realm while at the same time having a relationship with God in the spirit realm. The same things, interestingly enough, that stopped that first generation of Israelites from stepping into their Promised Land can also stop us today. There is a progression of advancement that Israel was taken through on their journey to inherit and live in God's promises.

Israel was first delivered from Egypt, then taken into the wilderness, and then eventually led into the Promised Land. Likewise, we as believers go through a very similar journey on the path to fully inheriting and living in God's promises for our lives. As believers, there is a moment in time when we are "delivered from Egypt." This takes place at the moment you are born again. You are delivered from the kingdom of darkness and transferred into the Kingdom of God's Son. At that moment of deliverance, you start a process of falling more in love with God and learning to give yourself over to Him in the realm of your soul, mind, will, and emotions. This, for a believer, is like the wilderness. The wilderness is where Israel was faced with issues of the soul. They were grateful for their deliverance from Egypt, but then had to face some of the hardships of the desert, and had to learn to put all their trust in God. Israel did not always pass that test. In fact, the wilderness became known as a time of great grumbling and complaining from Israel. This leads us to what I will share with you in this chapter. Israel responded to God in such a way that hindered an entire generation from entering into God's promises for them. May it not be so for us in our lives. Let's learn some lessons from Israel's wilderness wanderings, and come to a place of "soul-surrender" in our lives in such a way that launches us into our destinies!

All-Important Intimacy

What were some of the issues that held up the Israelites? The warning in Hebrews 3:6-17 is meant to apply to us, and the first issue is *lack of intimacy*.

Now I know this sounds too simple, and that's because it is. We must never forget the simplicity of intimacy with God in our lives. We have been created to be naturally supernatural, but where we go wrong as believers is to stop doing the little things right. There used to be a time when we were disciplined. There used to be a time when we would pray. We were so in love with Jesus. Now we are off to the next big conference revelation or the next big thing in the Christian world. As I have said before, living in the supernatural is all about maintenance. We must never forget the simple yet profound importance of connecting with God daily.

The Holy Spirit lovingly rebukes us with these words: *"They always go astray in their heart, and they have not known My ways"* (Heb. 3:10). This is the measuring rod of intimacy. If your relationship with God on an intimate level is beginning to suffer for whatever reason, the more it suffers, the harder and more closed off you will become to the things of the Spirit, because your Spirit is fed by communion with God. Your Spirit is fed by being in that place of intimacy with Him.

Now, I want to mention that there are seasons of your life where you will have been diligent in everything you should be diligent in. You will have continued to stay focused on God. But things are still dry in your spiritual life. Sometimes God is testing your faithfulness. Will you be faithful and do what you know you are supposed to do even when you do not feel His overwhelming Presence at every turn? Sometimes a wilderness season helps you to develop a good lovesickness for Him. You might not realize how badly you need God until you don't feel Him. God is calling you to dig deep into faithfulness to find those underground streams. They may not be watering holes for you yet, because you need to dig to find God in those times. But that is intimacy, too.

Pressing Through Unbelief

Another hindrance that got in the way of progress for the Israelites was unbelief: *"Take care, brothers, lest there be in any of you an evil, unbelieving heart, leading you to fall away from the living God....So we see that they were unable to enter because of unbelief"* (Heb. 3:12, 19 ESV).

Sometimes people want to live in the supernatural, but they cannot get over their own doubt and unbelief that it is available for them. We must get over our doubt and unbelief.

For some of us, this means that we have to "get over ourselves." That's one of the things the Lord told me years ago when I was struggling with some of these things. You too may struggle with not feeling worthy to enter into these kind of encounters. Why would God make this available? You may not feel like you live right. You must get over yourself, because sometimes you are the biggest obstacle to what God wants to do in your life. You must press through the disbelief and the doubt.

The Israelites were not able to enter into the Promised Land because they did not truly believe that God intended to wipe out the giants before them. They looked at everything that was around them in the natural realm and how all the cards seemed to be stacked against them, and they decided to put more faith in what they could see than in the power and promises of their God. When it really came down to it, they questioned God.

One thing that will close up your own spiritual senses is unbelief. Unbelief is "catching." So do not let the naysayers into your life. I have seen people who were following God just fine—until they began to surround themselves with others who were not really in favor of the direction God was leading them. So they back down and they start to question, "Do I really, really believe that? Is that true?"

Unbelief is the same as *lack of faith* or lack of confidence (see Heb. 3:14). Hebrews 11:6 tells us that it is impossible to please God without faith. When Jesus had just raised Lazarus from the dead, Jesus said to Lazarus' sister, Martha, "Did I not say to you that if you would only believe I would show you the glory of God?" (see John 11:40). Without faith in the unseen realm, your spiritual senses will close over.

Not only will unbelief (lack of faith) shut down your spiritual senses, but it can also allow you to lose your footing and slip into sin. Sin leads to a *hardened heart*, which is another reason we fail to live a fully supernatural life. Every time you miss the mark, every time you do something that you know is sin, without immediately repenting and turning your heart back to God, it causes another layer of hardness to come over your spiritual senses.

Sin is so easy, as simple as not obeying something the Lord asked you to do. When God asks you to do something and you do not do it, a layer of hardness will come over your heart, and the next time He speaks to you, His voice will seem fainter to you. If you continue the sin or if you disobey the Lord again, another layer of hardness will come over your heart, and another. Soon you will hear only a whisper. Before long, you will not be hearing Him at all. It is not God's fault and it is not that God is not speaking. It is that you have allowed your heart to become hardened, whether you did it intentionally or not. A hardened heart is not spiritually sensitive.

It is vitally important that we develop a lifestyle of "running to God" whenever we trip up in some area. Run to Him immediately! His blood provides immediate grace and forgiveness. It's when we trip up and then hide from

God that our hearts become hardened. Don't let the devil lie to you. God is a good Father and He loves it when His children run *to* Him, not *from* Him.

Overcoming Fear and Disobedience

Here's one thing that we do not usually think about: the *fear of deception*. As I mentioned earlier, fear of deception is putting your faith in the enemy. If you have an overwhelming fear of deception in your life, it will hinder and block your spiritual senses.

Some people think it is healthy to have a fear of deception, because it will keep them safe. But that is still operating out of fear rather than faith. You have not been given the spirit of fear. Fear is not of God (see 2 Tim. 1:7). However, *"perfect love casts out fear"* (1 John 4:18).

So if we believe that God's love for us is perfect, then why should we not trust Him to protect us as we learn and develop in the things of the Spirit. Jesus said, "Ask and it will be given to you. Seek and you will find. Knock and it will be opened to you. For everyone who asks, receives. And the one who seeks finds. And to the one who knocks it will be opened. Or which one of you if his sons asks him for bread will give him a stone? Or if he asks for a fish will give him a serpent? If you then who are evil know how to give good gifts to your children how much more will your Father who is in Heaven give good things to those who ask him?" (see Matt. 7:7-11).

Your Father has good plans for you. When you begin to learn to hear His voice and operate in the things of His Spirit, you have to believe that He is there to protect you. Your fear of deception can be one thing that will stop you from entering God's rest. *"To whom did He swear that they would not enter His rest but to those who were disobedient?"* (Heb. 3:18 ESV). *Disobedience* is another area that will prevent you from progressing in God every single time. Search your heart and ask God to search your heart to discover if there is any area in your life where you have not obeyed the Lord. Oftentimes, people get breakthrough when they come back to that surrendered place of obedience to God.

What's on Your Screen?

Your imagination or image center is vital to your ability to see and hear what God wants to show and tell you. Your image center is like a big blank movie screen, and God wants to put visions and words there for you to see. Some people, however, cannot use their image centers.

Each of us has stewardship of our image center. Some people choose ungodly things, such as sexual sin, lust, and pornography. Then every time they get quiet and try to listen to God, ungodly images come to mind. They do not know what to do, so they decide to *disdain the visionary* in order to avoid lust. They will avoid entering into quietness and stillness altogether, trying to avoid the lust that comes up in their hearts.

As a result, not only do they have a problem with ungodly images, but they also close themselves off to hearing from God. If you are struggling in some of these areas, I encourage you to uproot those images from your heart by seeking help from mature Christians. Don't disdain the whole visionary experience just because you are trying to avoid sin.

Other people have learned to disdain the visionary to avoid unpleasant memories. Some people have not been healed from traumatic experiences they had in the past. And the way they live their life today is still through the lens of how they were hurt or traumatized in the past. Every time they get quiet enough to enter into the visionary realm, all that comes up are those old traumas from their past. Soon, they too will learn to avoid quietness altogether, and as a result, their spiritual senses will not get used at all.

Staying Aligned With God

In order to experience a supernatural life, we must stay aligned with God. We have been listing the hindrances that can cause us to come out of alignment: *lack of intimacy, unbelief, fear of deception, disobedience,* and *disdaining the visionary,* and we need to add a few more.

Idolizing the rational. The way God communicates is not always rational to the natural mind. In fact, the Bible says the natural mind cannot discern it (see 1 Cor. 2:14). It can only be discerned spiritually. Your natural mind is always going to want to reason things through, and your desire to understand the rationale for everything can overpower your ability to be open to hear whatever He might say without having to understand it first. Focusing too strictly on rational matters will close off your spiritual senses.

The cares of the world. The Bible says that the cares of the world choke out the Word of God in your life and bring about unfruitfulness (see Mark 4:19). The proper response is to cast your cares and your anxieties upon the Lord (see 1 Pet. 5:7). Jesus will take your burdens for you. When we begin to worry and be anxious over things in our lives, then it becomes an issue of pride. That is like us saying that we don't fully trust God to take this burden, and if we worry about it enough, we can figure out a way to solve the problem. First Peter 5:6 says to *"humble yourself under the mighty hand of God"* and cast your anxieties upon Him. He loves you!

No hunger. Jesus says, *"Blessed are those who hunger and thirst for righteousness"* (Matt. 5:6). If you are not hungry for God, you need to ask God to make you hungry. First Corinthians 14:1 says, *"Earnestly desire the things of the Spirit."*

Unworthiness and insecurity. This is a big hindrance to spiritual freedom. Insecurity and unworthiness defeat us before we get started. They keep us from feeling that we can partner with God. Remember the spies whom Moses sent in to spy out the Promised Land? They reported how desirable the territory was. They also said "There are giants in the land. They are enormous! They're bigger than us. We were like grasshoppers in our own sight; therefore, we were like grasshoppers in their sight" (see Num. 13:33). In essence, they were convinced that "they will have us for lunch." They saw themselves as little and insignificant. Therefore, they were not about to step into what they thought was impossible, a death trap. Only Joshua and Caleb said otherwise. They said, "If God delights in us, then He will be with us and our enemies will be our bread" (see Num. 14:9). They were confident that God wanted the best for them, because they had a revelation that God delighted in them!

And as we know, they were only two Israelites of that generation who were allowed to enter the Promised Land forty long years later. Their confidence in God paid off. The other spies carried a spirit of fear, unworthiness, insecurity. But Joshua and Caleb were "of a different Spirit" (see Num. 14:24). They not only believed God, they recognized that victory did not depend upon their insufficient human strength.

Hopelessness, depression. These were also hindrances to conquering the Promised Land, just as they are when we try to break through to a higher level of spiritual living. Hopelessness and depression are two of satan's most effective strategies to hinder your spiritual senses and *intimacy with God.*

Not remembering God's faithfulness. This happened to the Israelites: *"But they soon forgot his works. They did not wait for his counsel. But they had a wonton craving in the wilderness and put God to the test in the desert. He gave them what they asked but sent a wasting disease among them"* (Ps. 106:13-15 ESV).

Never forget what God has done for you, lest you slide into discouragement and hopelessness. One of the things that will close up, block, and hinder your spiritual senses is when you forget what God has done for you and how He has brought you to where you are today.

You need to understand that every time God has done something in your life, any encounter you have had with Him means that He has invaded your time and space, He has broken through from the eternal realm into the realm of time. That includes when you were born again. When you were born again, He invaded your time and space and came into your life.

When you hear the voice of God or have any kind of an encounter with Him, those moments are doorways that remain open. They can give you access into future encounters with God. Nothing is ever stale in the Kingdom. You can read a Scripture, and ten years later get fresh revelation on it. You can recollect the experiences you have had with God in the past, and as you remind yourself of those times when He came from eternity into your time, it can become a doorway for you to have a fresh and brand-new experience with God. Those past encounters never become stale. God is always fresh.

On those days when you are just really struggling and feeling nothing, begin to remind yourself of what God has done for you in the past. Remind yourself of how He saved you, redeemed you, and lifted you up to be seated with Him. Remind yourself of how He has delivered you from things that kept you bound. Find something to praise God for, *no matter* how you feel. If you do this, you will quickly find yourself in such a place of genuine praise, worship, and thanksgiving that the presence of God will flood your heart!

Keys for Developing Spiritual Senses

We've talked about what hinders your spiritual senses, so now let's talk about what helps activate and develop your spiritual senses.

Do you believe that the supernatural realm is your inheritance? If you do not, you are not likely to develop your spiritual senses. The first key to developing your spiritual senses is to *believe that the supernatural realm is your inheritance in this life*. God communicates supernaturally. He is supernatural. You cannot have a relationship with Him outside of living in the supernatural. The primary key for developing your spiritual senses is simply your own desire and ability to claim your full inheritance. This is so important. You must believe that a supernatural lifestyle "belongs" to you as part of your reality as a new creation in Christ Jesus. Once you believe it, you have to contend for it by faith.

The second key is also foundational: *exercise your imagination*. You must fill your image center. David would lie on his bed at night meditating on the Lord. The prophets would spend time resting and pondering on the Lord. One way that I begin to activate my spiritual senses is to exercise my imagination by reading the parables of the Bible and the prophetic encounters. When I read about Ezekiel and the four living creatures or Abraham when the angels came to him, I spend time thinking about them. Dedicating my imagination to the Lord for His purposes, I try to picture those encounters. I let the words paint a picture in my mind. There are tons of things you could dedicate your imagination to. Why not dedicate it to the things of God?

The Bible tells you to *"set your mind on things above"* (Col. 3:2). More biblical advice: "Do not look at the things that are seen but look at the things that are unseen. For the things that are seen are transient" (see 2 Cor. 4:18). They are temporary. They are here today, gone tomorrow. If you look at the unseen, you are filling your image center with eternal images, and they are not transient; they are stable and strong. So do not waste your time or imagination thinking about the things of earth. Be heavenly minded. Maybe you've heard the phrase, "You are so heavenly minded that you are no earthly good." That is a lie. The fact is that if we as believers were more heavenly minded, we would be much more earthly good.

A third key for developing your spiritual senses is simply *waiting and soaking in the presence of God.* I went into depth on this topic in chapter four, *Stillness and Soaking.*

When you are waiting for Him, think of it as *soaking* in His presence:

> *The children of men take refuge in the shadow of Your wings. They drink their fill of the abundance of Your house; And You give them to drink of the river of Your delights. For with You is the fountain of life; In Your light we see light* (Psalm 36:7-9 NASB).

A fourth key is *Word meditation.* Word meditation will awaken your spiritual senses. The Word is like a lamp shining in a dark place. It is just a little lamp in a vast, dark place. But as you pay attention to it, it becomes like the morning star rising in your heart and the dawning of the new day (see 2 Pet. 1:19). Remember what we noted earlier: the more you meditate on the Word of God, the more you give your spiritual senses something for God to breathe on.

Another very important key is *consecration*. Samuel became a prophet in God's house because he had been consecrated to the Lord by his mother. You consecrate your life to God when you give Him the first fruits of your time in every area of your life. If you consecrate your spiritual senses to God and offer them up to God for Him to use, your very act of consecration will begin to awaken them.

Do not forget the importance of *worship*. Also simply being still. *"Be still, and know that I am God"* (Ps. 46:10). Gaze upon the Lord (see Heb. 12; Ps. 27:4). Think about Him; imagine being with the Lord.

You "build yourself up on your most holy faith" when you *pray in tongues* (see Jude 20-21). Paul said that when you pray in tongues your mind is unfruitful but your spirit is praying unto God. He said I will pray with my mind but I will also pray with my spirit (see 1 Cor. 14:14-15). Praying in tongues activates your spirit, which is equipped with your spiritual senses. Pray in tongues when you are driving to work. Pray in tongues all the way home. Force yourself to do it. It does not matter at all whether you want to or not. Force yourself to do it. Put some worship music on in the car and pray in tongues as you drive. When you pray in tongues, you are activating your Spirit.

We have touched already on most of these keys for developing your spiritual senses, but they are too important to forget. Here are some more: *Believe that you are seated in heavenly places* (see Eph. 2:5-6). That is reality. It does not matter how you feel when you wake up in the morning. From the moment you wake up in the morning until you put your head on the pillow at night, 24 hours a day, seven days a week, you are seated in heavenly places. One of the best things you can do to activate and sensitize your spiritual senses is to remind yourself in faith about this reality. Say to yourself, "I am seated right now with Christ in heavenly places." As you declare that truth, you will activate your spirit.

James reminds us that we have not because we ask not (see James 4:2). So—*ask.* Pray and ask God to open up your spiritual senses.

Act on your *hunger and desperation.* Expect God to come through for you. Do you remember the story about the prophet and the ditches? During a serious drought, the Word of the Lord came through a prophet, and he said, "Dig a bunch of ditches and God says He will fill them with rain." (See Second Kings 3:15-20.) I am sure the people did not operate in a high degree of faith, but they were desperately thirsty. In the same way, you will "dig a ditch" when you are desperate. You want God to fill those trenches with his Spirit. Digging a ditch is doing your due diligence no matter what you feel coming from God's direction. You do not expect Him to do something first, but instead *you* do something first. You make your life an airstrip for God to land on. Desperate people do not care what anybody else says. People told blind Bartimaeus to be quiet. But instead he cried out even more (see Mark 10:46-52). He did not care how he was viewed by anyone else. He knew the Son of God was walking by, and he was a desperate man. Ask God to make you desperate, too.

Pure in Heart

The Bible says that the pure in heart will see God (see Matt. 5:8). *Holiness and purity* matter. Remember the Zadok priesthood (see Ezek. 44:15). God told them that because they had remained loyal to Him, they could have free and open access to walk into His most holy place. As we remain loyal and pure, He will give us free and open access into the things of the Spirit, into His most holy place, to His very throne. The writer of Hebrews exhorts us to *"come boldly to the throne of grace"* (Heb. 4:16). And the world will once again discern the difference between the holy and the profane through you.

Holiness is not about obeying a list of rules and regulations. You do not have to get things right before you can come to God. But that is often what has been preached. That breeds a performance mentality: if you have performed well enough to keep those impurities out of your life, then you can get closer to God. If you have not performed well enough to keep those things out of your life, then you can't come closer to God. But that is not the Gospel of the New Covenant. That is not the Gospel of the Kingdom.

You *can* come to God with all of your baggage. You can come to God with all of your mess. You can *"come boldly before the throne of grace"* in your time of desperation and need. Instead of obeying a bunch of rules, holiness means you are carrying around a bunch of baggage yet you are allowed by the grace of God to come close to Him. Then you begin to realize some of the baggage does not feel right anymore and does not satisfy the way it used to. Out of love (not legalism), you throw it away.

Ask for Awakened Senses

The last key to activating and developing your spiritual senses is to *Ask*. James 4:2 says: *"You do not have because you do not ask."* It's time to present your spiritual senses to God and ask Him to activate and energize them. What you present and offer up to God is what He will use in your life. Romans 6:13 says *"Do not present your members as instruments of unrighteousness to sin, but present yourselves to God as being alive from the dead, and your members as instruments of righteousness to God."* Present your senses to God today, that we might be slaves to righteousness and live in heavenly realms daily. It's your inheritance!

After learning to activate and sensitize your spiritual senses, you will begin to experience the flow of God's Spirit in your life. Read on as I explain some of the different types of encounters that you can expect and believe for in your life.

Chapter 7

Supernatural Experiences "On Earth as It Is in Heaven" Part 1

In the Old Testament, Joel prophesied, *"And it shall come to pass afterward that I will pour out My Spirit on all flesh; your sons and your daughters shall prophesy, your old men shall dream dreams, your young men shall see visions"* (Joel 2:28).

We have been born into the times about which he spoke, and everyone who has God's Spirit, young or old, male or female, can receive revelation straight from God. In this chapter I will be focusing on receiving revelation through what we call the "seer realm" or sensory encounters; and in the next chapter, I will get into the realm of angelic visitations and auditory manifestations of God's presence.

Many people have been schooled to receive revelation in the form of verbal statements from the Holy Spirit. Others have learned to interpret dreams or understand visions. Let me state up front that I do not believe that one method for receiving God's communications is better than any others. No model is the higher or better model. It is all the Voice of God, in one way or another, being communicated.

I sometimes see a jostling or a competition when it comes to prophetic encounters, as people are learning to open up to the supernatural. For example, someone will say, "Well, I was reading the Word the other day and a Scripture just kind of jumped out at me, and I got this revelation. The Lord spoke this to me." Then someone else will say, "Well, I had an open-eyed vision, you know, and I got the revelation." The next person will say, "I had an angel walk into the room, slap me upside the head, blow a trumpet in my face, and give me the message." But each person got pretty much the same revelation as the other person. We need to value the message itself, regardless of how it was packaged.

What's on the Menu?

Revelation is revelation. We are not to rate revelation based on how it comes, and it does not mean you can consider yourself better or worse than anyone else because you get revelation in different ways. God will speak to you in some ways more often than in others.

But do not get stuck in a rut. In other words, do not say, "Well, this is how God uses me, this is how God has always used me, and I don't ever see visions," or whatever. It may be true that you do not often see visions, but you should be open to the possibility.

Every person has spiritual senses, even though you will find that you use some senses more readily than others. You never hear people say, "I can use my feet, but I'm better at using my hands, so I just don't use my feet." You may not be a carpenter, but you can use your hands anyway, and you do. It is the same with our spiritual senses. In the same way you interact with the natural realm through your five natural senses, you can also interact with God and His spiritual realm through your spiritual senses of seeing, hearing, smelling, touching, and tasting.

Jesus instructed us to pray that it would be on earth as it is in Heaven. Do we really believe that it can be in our life as it is in Heaven? I don't talk about it much because my primary focus is always on God, but quite often I feel angels in meetings where I am ministering; they will sometimes touch me on my shoulder or in some other way. When this happens, it causes me to really tune in to what God is doing in the unseen realm, much like Elisha tuned into the unseen realm when the Syrian army was coming after him (see 2 Kings 6:8-23). We shared that story in the last chapter. This should be normal for us. We don't worship angels, but they are in Heaven and we should believe for our lives to be heavenly, so why not believe for the activity of God's angels in our lives?

Many times throughout the Old Testament you will read that the prophets would say, "I felt the hand of the Lord God come upon me." Maybe it was the hand of the Lord, or maybe it was one of His angels. Regardless of where it came from, it is a real touch.

Likewise, regardless of how your physical auditory or visual or olfactory organs are used—or not—you will hear real sounds and see or smell real things. All of this is part of the experience of the seer realm, God's unseen spiritual realm.

Learning about these things is like going to a restaurant and looking at the menu. When you look at that menu, you can see everything that is available for you to order. I cannot tell you about every different kind of encounter you can have with God. But I can describe many very common experiences, along with a few that are much more *un*common. It's important that we know what is legally and biblically available for us as believers according to the Word of God.

Open Heavens

Now that we are living in New Covenant times, the heavens are open all the time, but in the Old Testament, the heavens opened only once in a while. The New Testament theology of open heavens is that the heavens have been opened since Jesus died and rose from the dead. His death in the flesh opened up that *"new and living way"* to Heaven for us forever, never to be closed again (see Heb. 10:20).

Jesus has opened the heavens for us, but not every believer is living under the open Heaven. Just because He paid for it to open up does not mean you and I are living by it. You can be in a meeting where one person is receiving openly and freely from the Lord, yet the person in the next seat may be feeling nothing. We have an enemy that tries to release oppressive atmospheres over us personally, over our families, churches, cities, and nations, and even over whole continents. Satan will do whatever he can to hinder you from accessing the heavens that are open and laying hold of your full inheritance.

Ezekiel had some extreme, incredible encounters with God. If you pay attention to the kinds of encounters Ezekiel had, you can glean some important nuggets about the seer dimension. He writes, "In the thirtieth year, and the fourth month, on the fifth day of the month as I was among the exiles by the River Chabar, the heavens were opened and I saw visions of God" (see Ezek. 1:1). Other people were all around Ezekiel by the River Chabar, but they do not seem to have entered into this encounter, nor did they see any of it.

He goes on: *"As I looked, behold, a stormy wind came..."* (Ezek. 1:4 ESV). Stop and notice what he said there: *"As I looked...."* You will see it every single time the prophets had an encounter with God. For the prophets, looking was an intentional thing. They were not forced into some encounter. They felt the hand of the Lord God, and when they felt it, they immediately postured themselves to receive from Him.

Ezekiel looked. *"As I looked, behold, a stormy wind came out of the north, and a great cloud, with brightness around it, and fire flashing forth continually, and in the midst of the fire, as it were gleaming metal. And from the midst of it came the likeness of four living creatures. And this was their appearance..."* (Ezek. 1:4-5 ESV). Needless to say, Ezekiel finds himself in the midst of a vision—an awesome vision with living creatures that had four faces each, wings with little human arms underneath, blinking eyeballs all over their bodies, etc.

He was sitting amongst a bunch of people and he entered into a vision in which he could see things and hear sounds. One moment his senses were filled with the river and the people around him and the atmosphere of the place, and the next moment he was seeing and hearing incredible things in the unseen realm. This unseen spiritual realm was and is just as real as the natural realm that Ezekiel was sitting in with the captives. He did not experience this with his natural senses; he experienced it in his spirit, with his spiritual senses.

Ezekiel heard a voice. *"And he said to me, 'Son of man, stand on your feet and I will speak with you....You, son of man, hear what I say to you. Be not rebellious like that rebellious house; open your mouth and eat what I give you.' And when I looked, behold, a hand was stretched out to me, and behold, a scroll of a book was in it"* (Ezek. 2:1,8 ESV).

You must understand that Ezekiel is still in a vision. Nothing has become tangible in the natural realm at this point, but he talks about everything as if it were real. It *is* real; it is completely real. It is just in a different dimension. For years I have had a friendship with an incredible prophet in the Body of Christ who operates in the seer dimension. When I first met him, I was frustrated about how he defined reality. He is a very sensory oriented prophet. We spent some time together in the early days. He would say, "The Angel of the Lord was just here."

And I would say, "How do you know?"

And he would say, "Because I smelled him."

Immediately, I wanted to know *how* he smelled the angel—did he smell him in the spirit or in the natural? How did this work?

Or he would say, "I saw him," or "There was a flash of light."

I would always ask, "What do you mean? Did you see that flashing light in your mind's eye or did you see it with your physical eyes?"

He would always look at me and say, "Boy, what difference does it make?"

I can be persistent. So the next time I was over there I asked him again. I wanted a better answer, but what I got was a loving rebuke. Essentially, he said to me, "You want the answer to that question because if I tell you that I had a vision in my head, you would think it was less real than if a flash of light and an angel came into my room, picked up my Bible, and smacked me across the head." He was right. At that time in my life I placed a higher value on the natural realm, as if it were more legitimate. I thought that if something happened in the unseen realm, it could be pretend, made up.

God began to convict me about my lack of faith. He spoke to me about how everything that I see on the earth comes from the invisible realm.

Visible Reality and Invisible Reality

I could now tell you that supernatural things are just as real as physical ones, but when you get down to it, the invisible realm is *more* real than the visible realm. Our physical senses can pick up quite a bit, but even in the physical realm, just think how much is invisible—sound waves or ozone, for example. The question becomes, "So what is reality?" We can no longer say that reality is only what we see. We can no longer say reality is only what we hear with our ears. Unseen and unheard reality is all around us, and we will be making a big mistake if we disregard it.

In fact, we need to learn to place value on the reality of the supernatural. Do not just try to be cool by saying that angels are around—they are really here. They are always around. Besides, the unseen realm and the visible realm are interrelated, so angels who are invisible to you can be right with you in physical space. Everything that has substance came from something that is unseen. God created the earth and everything in it from invisible nothingness. Even the chair you may be sitting on was first a thought in someone's mind before it was created.

In Ezekiel's case, he saw a scroll in a vision, and God told him, "Open your mouth and eat it." There was nothing tangible to this imaginary, visionary scroll, nor to the hand that was stretched out holding it. It was spread out before him, and it had writing on the front and the back; it was part of the prophetic word God was giving to the nation. And the voice said, "*'Son of man, eat whatever you find here. Eat this scroll and go, speak to the house of Israel.' So I opened my mouth, and he gave me this scroll to eat. And he said to me, 'Son of Man…fill your stomach with it.' Then I ate it, and it was in my mouth as sweet as honey*" (Ezek. 3:1-3 ESV). Here you see the moment where Ezekiel responded in faith to something that was intangible, something that he ingested invisibly—and it manifested in his mouth with a real, physical taste. That may sound crazy, but it is really not.

That scroll that was invisible was just as real as a physical scroll would have been. It's just as if Ezekiel ate sweet-tasting paper. Do we believe the invisible realm is that real? This is a bit of a challenge, isn't it? But if we do not believe that, then by default, we have to question a lot of the things that we do believe. It would throw everything into question, that we believe about God. The unseen is real, even more real than the seen.

Fast-forward to Ezekiel 8, and we see Ezekiel in his house with the elders of Judah. He was hosting them; they were his guests. Suddenly he felt the hand of the Lord God. Again, he says, *"Then I looked,"* and he completely tuned out all of the elders, because God always takes priority. Ezekiel goes on to describe another vision of a startling individual, and we have no indication that the elders of Judah saw any of this, although they were sitting in the same room with Ezekiel. (Was it not real because they were not able to see it? You have to ask yourself questions like this.)

In a vision, *"He put out the form of a hand and took me by a lock of my head"* (Ezek. 8:3 ESV). This still was not physical, because the next verse describes how the Spirit lifted him up between earth and Heaven and brought him in visions of God, to Jerusalem. What happened is that he was taken out of his body and brought to Jerusalem in the spirit.

The Spirit took Ezekiel to Jerusalem, and brought him to the entrance of the court. Again he looked (still in the spirit) and he observed a hole in the wall (see Ezek. 8:7). *"Son of Man,"* said the voice, *"dig in the wall."* This is fascinating, because he was not there physically, and yet God's Spirit was telling him to dig in the wall. I have to chew on that one. Somehow, he dug a hole in the wall and entered.

Meanwhile, remember, his body was still sitting there in front of the elders of Judah. They must have been watching him. All of this is a good illustration of the blending of visible and invisible realities, and it is a good argument for being open to such experiences.

Why is it that we get so scared about New Age astral-projection and those kinds of things? If anything, what should bother us is that the devil is getting glory for something that God created. If that sort of thing scares you, then you are being frightened by something that God created. I say that very boldly. If traveling in the spirit realm scares you, then you are scared of something God created. The devil did not create it. The devil only utilizes something that God created, and he finds a way to teach people how to do it illegally. And people can do it without obeying God, because we were all made with the capacity to interact in the spiritual dimension, and we were all created to be naturally supernatural. Even if you do not worship Jesus and you do not have God living within you and you have not been born again, you can still function in supernatural realms.

It is possible to engage the supernatural without the help of the Holy Spirit—but those who do are operating illegally and outside of the Kingdom of God. They are operating in the spirit realm illegally, not God's way. Satan used to be one of the most powerful angels in Heaven; he is supernatural and he understands the ways of the spirit realm. He can make it possible for people who are not born again to travel out of their bodies in the spirit. Just because this scares some people does not mean we can decide that it is not true.

Sensory Experiences of the Unseen Realm

Let me now begin to just describe some of the various experiences that are available to you as a believer and that many in the Bible experienced as well. In a moment of boasting, Paul wrote, *"I must go on boasting. Though there is nothing to be gained by it, I will go on to visions and revelations of the Lord"* (2 Cor. 12:1 ESV). Notice that he uses the plural: "visions" and "revelations," more than one of each, and, as we know, of various types.

What are some of the different kinds of experiences people can have with the Lord? I want to start with the *sense of smell,* because I want to share a funny story with you. In the spirit, the sense of smell was one of the last spiritual senses to be activated in my life. I had visions and other experiences, but I had never smelled anything in the spirit. I had been at meetings where someone would say, "Do you smell that? It smells like roses!"

They were smelling a heavenly scent in a supernaturally natural way.

I would always have to say, "No I don't smell that." This would happen all the time. It got kind of irritating to me, in a healthy way, because I wanted the same experience. Not for the sake of chasing an experience, but because I have a healthy hunger for all that God desires me to have in my life.

After a while, I was part of a four-day intensive school in which a friend was teaching. At one point, my friend stopped his session because he felt that a "God moment" was imminent. Somebody began to play music, and I went up on the balcony to get alone with God. Suddenly, someone started yelling, "Can you smell that?"

Forgetting about my dignity, I rushed down from the balcony and walked right out into the middle of the platform, because I was one of the ministry team. There were about six hundred people there, but I didn't care what they thought. I wanted to experience this smell. Sure enough, I did. There were powerful fragrances being blown back and forth across the stage. First, I detected the strongest scent of pine, then a flowery smell, and then the aroma of incense. As the fragrances continued on the stage, the fragrance was moving through the crowd. Row by row, you could hear people uttering "Uh, uh, uh," as it moved. We asked for a show of hands as to how many people were smelling these various scents, and over 90 percent of the people were smelling it. It was a tangible visitation of fragrances from Heaven, which are better than anything you have ever smelled before on earth. Those were the strongest fragrances I had ever smelled, and ever since then, it's as if that particular sense has been awakened for me.

Since that time, I can be in my hotel room preparing for a meeting, and the fragrance of His presence will roll into the room. It doesn't happen all the time, and I don't seek after it, but I sure love when God does it. A common manifestation of this spiritual sense in my life today is often used in the work of deliverance. The smell that sometimes fills a room when the demons come out of a person during a deliverance session is just horrific. Sometimes when I am in a ministry setting, people will come up to me and ask for ministry and I will smell that smell. I have found that normally it is an indication that God wants them to be delivered right then and there; they are ready and so is He. You must be open to sense the dark dimensions of the unseen realm as well, because as believers we are called to invade the darkness with light!

A more commonplace spiritual sense is what we can call *spiritual perception*. An example of this can be found in Mark 2:8. Spiritual perception is like a gut feeling in your spirit, an impression in your spirit. Jesus actually rebuked people based only on this kind of a gut feeling. All the time, Jesus said things like, "I sense within," "I perceive," and "I know."

Sometimes people get overwhelming gut feelings that they should not do something. People's lives have been saved because they obeyed an overwhelming feeling that they should not go on a certain road on a certain day, or if they had, they would have been involved in a terrible pile-up accident. The Holy Spirit communicates directly to our spirits. We have learned not to ignore the feelings and senses that we perceive with our natural bodies. We must also learn not to ignore the feelings and senses that we perceive with our spirit.

Different Kinds of Visions

Visions are unique and distinctive experiences and they fall into several categories. In the Greek language, seven or eight different words are used for different kinds of visions. In English, we must add adjectives to achieve the same degree of clarity. We just use the word "vision." But in the New Testament times, specifically in the Book of Acts, visions were such a common way for God to speak, there were several different words to describe each kind of vision. Here are the most common kinds of visions.

Pictorial vision. A pictorial vision is very simple: it is like a snapshot or a still photo in your mind. Sometimes, a pictorial vision appears as if you superimposed a photo over a natural object. For example, oftentimes when the Lord wants me to prophesy over someone, I will see an image in my mind, superimposed over the person in front of me. I see these things in my mind, not in the natural, but they seem to be superimposed over a person. Often I will see a Scripture, a color, or any variety of other things. It's simply the Holy Spirit giving me directions for ministry. God also uses this when I move in the gift of Word of Knowledge for healing and miracles. I will often have snapshot visions in my mind of people's body parts or of a certain person's face or name. I act upon what I see, and call those things out, and as people respond, healing begins to take place.

Panoramic vision. This is a pictorial vision that is in motion. Everybody can do this with the imagination. For instance, you can see yourself driving down the road in your car with landmarks going by. A panoramic vision is what Ananias had when the Lord told him to walk to the street called Straight and pray over Saul of Tarsus, who was up until then a murderer of Christians (see Acts 9:10-16). Also, Saul's encounter right before that on the road to Damascus was a panoramic vision. A bright light knocked him onto the dirt, and out of the light a Voice said, *"I am Jesus whom you are persecuting"* (Acts 9:5).

When Peter was on the rooftop and the white sheet came down from Heaven in Acts 10:9-16, that was a panoramic vision. He may have seen it deep in his mind's eye, or it may have appeared to him as if it were on a movie screen. This experience that Peter had in a vision, literally opened up the entire Gentile world as a harvest field. If you are not a Jew and you are a born-again believer, then you are saved today because Peter had a vision of a white sheet coming down from Heaven and was told to eat the four-footed animals on the sheet. I know it sounds weird and strange, but the Holy Spirit speaks in mysterious ways. Thank God that the Book of Acts believers were open to all forms of hearing from God! For those of us who have denied these types of encounters or labeled them as New Age, this would be a good time to humble ourselves and repent for disregarding the precious ways that God speaks to His people.

If you have never had a vision like this, do not be worried about the risk of engaging in enemy-directed "visualization." Yes, the enemy does counterfeit these kinds of visions, but we cannot let that stop us from receiving the genuine visionary experiences that God has created and designed for us. If the Spirit of God initiates it, it is real spirit realm communication, and it is important.

Open-eye vision. This is when you see something with your spiritual eyes (your imagination in your mind), but it is out in front of your wide-open natural eyes. In this kind of vision, you do not see every detail, and you do not always see things in full color. Sometimes, for example, when you see an angel, you will see an illumination, or just a shape or form. In contrast, in a *closed-eye vision* your eyes are closed, yet you can see something in front of you.

Dreams. The only difference between a dream and a vision is that a dream happens when you're asleep and a vision happens when you're awake. For some people, whose souls are so restless throughout the day that they can never quiet themselves enough to hear or see God, dreams are the best way to hear God. God can invade their dreams when their soul is finally quiet. Other people have a lot of dreams because it is a gifting on their life. God speaks through dreams, often symbolically. Revelation from dreams can be just as profound as revelation coming from visions.

Don't Limit God

The kinds of encounters we just discussed were common for New Testament believers in the Book of Acts, and they should be common for believers today. As I said at the beginning of this chapter, the outpouring that the Prophet Joel prophesied is upon us today! It is for you and it is for me. I pray that so far this book is challenging you to move with the cloud of God and advance deeper into what He created you for in His glory. Now, let's move forward into the next chapter as I share part two of *Supernatural Experiences "On Earth as It Is in Heaven."*

Chapter 8

Supernatural Experiences
"On Earth as It Is in Heaven"
Part 2

I was in Africa once when a friend of mine was doing a crusade in Kampala, Uganda. We showed up early, about thirty minutes before it started, and already about 55,000 people were waiting there. They had started gathering under the hot African sun at two o'clock in the afternoon for the crusade that started at seven. All afternoon, the worship team had been playing music and the people had been worshipping the Lord.

After I arrived, I was standing on the platform, when all of a sudden, I heard all 55,000 people go "Aah!" (and it is quite something to hear 55,000 people do that at one time). All of them, kids and adults, were looking up into the sky behind me to my right. I looked too. Up in the sky behind me, I saw an oval-shaped formation of a rainbow. I had never before seen anything like it, and I have never seen such a thing since. The colors of a rainbow appeared in an oval shape in the sky, like an opening. It looked like a divine hand had opened a hole in the demonic, oppressive atmosphere over the region.

It stayed in the sky for about fifteen minutes. From the moment we first saw it, miracles began to break out in the crowd. No one from the front had to say anything. No one touched the microphone.

Sovereignly, blind eyes started opening, the deaf started hearing, demons started coming out of people all over the place. The ushers were going crazy. They had to run out through the crowd because demons were coming out and people were flailing and screaming and hitting other people. The ushers had to get them and drag them out to a tent called the "deliverance tent." There were far too many to cast out one by one, so they just lay them there, and the Holy Spirit cast the demons out of them. For fifteen minutes it was like all of Heaven came down, and then it started to fade away.

As I stated earlier in this book, the heavens are open to all believers because of the death, resurrection, and ascension of Jesus. However, there is a devil that tries to establish hard oppressive atmospheres, empowered by people's sin, over cities and regions. This moment in Africa was a moment where God sovereignly broke through that oppressive atmosphere and demonstrated His Kingdom on earth as it is in Heaven! This kind of demonstration, the types of encounters that I spoke of in the last chapter, and the encounters I will speak of in this chapter, are all available to us as Christians today, in *this life,* as we believe for God's Kingdom to be on earth as it is in Heaven!

Angelic Visitations

Building on the previous chapter, I want to describe some more items on the spiritual "menu"—potential encounters of Spirit-to-spirit communication with God. One of those is angelic visitations. Angelic visitations or appearances feature prominently in the Bible, and they happen today more often than you might realize. I have had many different angelic encounters, and the more I grow with God, the more they have become quite common, although I do not treat them as common.

In the New Testament, you will remember, an angel appeared next to the priest Zachariah at the altar when he was serving in the temple (see Luke 1). Whether he saw the angel in the natural or in the spirit, it was an intense, tangible experience.

Sometimes, it can be a *very* tangible experience. I remember several years ago when I was in the basement of our home, in one of the rooms down there. I had a time of ministry coming up, and I was just spending time with the Lord. When I pray (or preach), I pace back and forth, so I was walking up and down the room as if it were a runway. My wife Kelly knows not to come into the room when I am in there praying.

I had gotten to the end of my "runway" when suddenly, right in front of me, was an angel so real that at first I thought I was seeing it with my natural eyes. The presence of this angel was so powerful that it went beyond a vision. It touched almost every one of my senses: my sense of touch, smell, hearing, everything. Nothing like this had ever happened before. The presence and power coming off this angel was so powerful that I could not stand it. I could not stand up at all; I just crumpled down onto the floor.

I wept for about an hour, and the angel never said anything the whole time. I knew that this was an angel saturated with the very presence of the Lord, and I ended up crawling on my hands and knees to the chair in the room. During this entire time, it wasn't even the angel that spoke to me. I was having a conversation with God. Having conversation with God often includes the experiences of "on earth as it is in Heaven." About that time, Kelly just came walking into the room. She just opened the door and came walking into the room about two or three feet with a question coming out of her mouth. She had forgotten that I was praying.

The room was filled with a literal mist; that is how tangible the presence of God was. You could see where it stopped; it didn't quite fill the whole room. Kelly walked about two feet into the room and hit that cloud of God's presence, and immediately she couldn't talk anymore and tears just started *shooting* out of her eyes. I have never seen her cry like that. Normally tears might stream down, but this time they just shot out of her eyes. I was a mess already myself.

All she could say was, "What's going on in here?"

And all I could say was, "It's an angel."

And she said, "I know, he's standing behind me," because she could feel the electricity running up and down her spine where the angel was standing. "I'll come back later," she said and she walked out of the room.

That was a tangible visitation similar to what Zechariah experienced in the temple. I love those, and I yearn for them. I believe in God without them because I live by faith, but I love it when something that real occurs.

The Father sent angels to minister to Jesus. If it is supposed to be on earth as it is in Heaven, and if Jesus in me is the Gateway of Heaven, then I want to have it right here in my life as it is in Heaven. Angels and blessing and favor and peace and God's presence are in Heaven. I want those things to be around me here on earth. That is a biblical desire.

I remember another time when God was teaching me how to move in the supernatural, and I still had this idea that angelic encounters and supernatural realm experiences were external-type events. I thought an angel would have to walk into my room and smack me upside the head and blow a trumpet in my face. It seemed unattainable and unrealistic.

I was about to go minister at a church, and I kept asking the Lord what He wanted me to say to the people. Every time I asked Him, this vision would pop in my mind of an angel dressed like a pioneer; he was just standing there. I did not know it was an angel. I thought I needed to get more sleep or something. I would toss it out. And then it happened again a few days later. Finally, on the evening before I was to minister, the vision happened again. This time, I dared to ask God to explain something about this to me. I allowed that image back into my mind. I know

now that I was peering into the spirit realm. But as a freewill agent, I was free to shut it all down, to shut my spiritual eyes. Your spiritual eyes are in the image center of your brain. I looked at the image and I said, "God, if this is You, breathe on this." At that moment, this angel began to speak, although it did not come of the form of him opening his mouth and speaking to me. Spontaneous thoughts began to flood my spirit and my mind.

The angel said to me: "I'm the angel who has been assigned to this place for this period of time. And this church is called to be a pioneering church." His being dressed as a pioneer was part of his message. And he said, "I want you give a prophetic word to the leader. I want you to tell him that in such-and-such a year [he told me the year], the leader had an encounter with God that pulled him out of marketplace work into five-fold minis-try work. I want you to tell them that, by December of this year, the people who have been coming against them are going to come and repent to them."

This was one of the first angelic encounters I had ever had, and the angel appeared in my mind's eye, giving me dates, details, and timeframes. I objected to God. I said, "God, I am not stepping out on this at all. This is not fair. I asked you for angelic encounters and this is not what I meant. This is not what I had in mind. I wanted the angel to come in here and sit down with me and talk to me." That was my perception of how it would have happened in the Bible.

My perception was wrong. The Lord simply said to me, "Well, this is what I've asked you to do in the meeting, and either you do it or I'm not going to break through in that meeting as I would like to." So, I went and I was obedient. I did not tell them how I got the word, but I delivered the word and it was right on. The year was exact, and then they called me and said, "Last month in December, we got these out-of-the-blue phone calls from people who called and repented for the backbiting they had done over the past two years."

And God showed up in that meeting. We had miracles and deliverance and healings. The demonstration of the Kingdom would not have happened apart from my obedience after I experienced that spirit-to-spirit angelic communication and revelation. These two angelic encounters are just two of many that I have experienced in my life as I have learned to live in the reality of God's presence and glory that has been given to us as believers.

God's Cloud of Glory

God would often visit people in a tangible way in the Bible where His "cloud of glory" would be seen and tangibly felt. This happened to the priests in First Kings 8:10-11. They tangibly experienced the cloud of God's glory. Again, Paul says in Second Corinthians that if Moses experienced such glory under a covenant of law and death, that his face shone with radiant light....then how much more of a surpassing glory we should experience under the New Covenant of life and the Spirit (see 2 Cor. 3:7-18). Any glory encounters that occurred in the Old Testament are still available to us today!

One day I had ten or twelve people watching TV at my house, and a cloud of God's glory rolled over into part of the room. It started raining in my part of the living room. I looked up at the ceiling and there were no drips. I said, "It's raining in here. It's raining on me." The others, who were people that I had spent time with, all looked at me as if to say, "Come *on*, Ryan. . . "

All I could say was, "Guys, my goodness, it's raining on me. I'm telling you, it's raining on me." As soon as I said that, a mist rolled over the other section of the room. It rolled over the couch. You could see with your natural eyes, and you could put your hand into it and pull it out and feel the wetness. By the end, it had rained on every single person sitting on the sectional couch.

You could feel the presence of God. Everyone was freaking out.

There was another period of my life when God was really jumpstarting my ministry training. He visited me for two and a half months, where often His tangible cloud of glory would visit me.

I love that side of God. He wants to touch our reality. Do we really believe that God still moves today like He did in Bible times? I believe He does and the Bible says He does too!

In the Bible, you can read about all kinds of heavenly visitations. John wrote the Book of Revelation to tell us about a lengthy visitation of the Lord. Moses had many encounters with God Himself, starting with his burning bush experience (see Exod. 3:3). Encounters with God range from the Old Testament to the New Testament and into today. *"Jesus Christ is the same yesterday, today and forever"* (Heb. 13:8)!

The realm of the spirit is filled with sensory experiences. I have experienced angels coming into a room, bringing light with them, as if flashbulbs were going off all over. They would pop and shoot across the room. Is this something like what Ezekiel saw when he said angels were moving like lightening across the sky? (See Ezekiel 1:13.) I didn't hear the thundering or the other things that Ezekiel heard, but I saw the flashes of light. Aren't we seated with Christ in heavenly places? (See Ephesians 2:6.) We believe for the effects of salvation to be experienced in this life, but why is it that believers don't believe for the effects of being seated in heavenly places with Christ to be experienced in this life?

These experiences give us a divine glimpse of what is going on in the spirit all the time. This stuff is happening all the time in the unseen realm around us, even right where you are this moment.

Trances

A trance is a state of being that prepares you for an experience. The trance itself is not really an experience. The trance is just kind of a heightened sensitivity to the spirit realm and a lowered sensitivity to the natural realm. Sometimes when you go into a trance you become so numb to the surroundings around you in the natural, you do not know if you're sitting or standing. You just kind of forget where you are because you are so in tune with the Spirit. It is kind of like a Holy Ghost anesthetic. Peter had a trance on the rooftop, and during the trance, he had a vision (see Acts 10:9-11). Because Peter had a vision in a trance on a rooftop, it led him to take the Gospel to the gentiles for the first time!

The first time I ever had a trance, I was ministering in a large city and my wife and I were in a hotel room. Kelly was working on the computer at the desk, and I had decided to lie down for a while. I thought I had fallen asleep, but I had not. My head had barely hit the pillow. I did not have time to fall asleep. I do not fall asleep that quickly. As soon as my head hit the pillow, I was unaware of anything else around me and I was in this visionary place. A pregnant girl walked up to me and told me her name and things about herself, and then she just faded away. The Lord then began to tell me what to do. He said that if I would call this girl out by name in the meeting, He would minister to her a sign, and a wonder would come from it.

So at the next meeting, I called this girl out. I did not know who she was. I didn't know if she would even be there, and the meeting was a small one, but I called out the name and she came forward. As it turned out, she was not literally pregnant, but the Lord had told me that she was pregnant with potential, although she was going the opposite direction. Sure enough, she hardly ever came to church. She was about eighteen or nineteen, living with two men, and far away from God.

When she came up, I began to prophesy to her about her potential and her destiny in God and how she would have to turn around or she would miss her destiny. As I was saying that, I could feel the glory of God come from behind me. It moved right through me, and when it hit me, I just began to weep. I was still trying to talk to this girl and tell her these amazing things God had told me about her, and God decided to touch her. The glory of God moved through me and touched her and she fell out under the power of God. I did not touch her. No one touched her. God did it. Then the glory of God began to move through the crowd. As the presence of God would hit each row, you could see the people begin to weep. You could tell where the glory of God was moving. It moved to about eight or ten rows back, and then it stopped. Nobody past that point seemed to be affected.

So I thought, "That was amazing," and we went on with the meeting. At the end of the meeting, the sign and wonder happened. A woman walked up to me and said, "I am the most powerful witch in all of East Village, Manhattan." I remembered having seen her in about the tenth row. She said, "Everybody knows me. I am a palm reader. When you were speaking tonight and you would talk about the things of God, there was this blue light that would come out of your mouth and it would fill the atmosphere in the room. What touched that girl? Because it came back and it stopped at my row. I know spiritual power. I have operated in spiritual power from the time I was a child. But that was incredible. Do you think that maybe it was love… ?" She said, "I have never felt love. But after feeling that, I have to know this Jesus." She got saved right there, that night!

The Audible Voice of God

We can learn to distinguish between an interior, voice-like "knowing" and a voice—or other sounds—perceived with our natural ears. Sometimes we can hear an inner audible sound, such that we do not know whether we have heard it with our physical ears or not. Most of the time, I do not hear an audible voice, but often enough I hear other audible sounds.

For example, I have been busy doing something in my hotel room, and I will hear knocking on my door. Of course, I go to the door and open it. Nobody's there! It happens again. Nobody's there again. By now, I should know this—God is knocking. He wants my attention. Or I will hear a bell going off, like a dinner bell, a real audible sound. Sometimes when I have heard it, other people with me have heard it as well, and at other times, the other people did not hear it.

I heard the audible voice of God for the first time when I was a teenager. I had gotten lost in the Bighorn Mountains on a backpacking trip. A snowstorm was coming at that elevation, and the rescuers said they would not be able to try to find me. The Red Cross said they would come in and get my body the next day. I had fallen into the river, and I was going into the early stages of hypothermia, but I was not at the stage of being out of my mind. In fact, I was thinking pretty clearly. I realized I was going to die.

At that time of my life, I had not been walking with God like I should have been. I remember praying, "God, if You will save me, I'll give my life to You in full-time ministry." I don't know why I said that; I sure didn't mean to say it. The thought was not even in my head, as far as I know. But when you are desperate, your heart speaks before your head gets involved. As soon as I said that, I audibly heard the Lord. All I heard was, "OK." And before the snow hit, a rescue team found me. They had been about to give up, but they had gotten together to pray one more time. Meantime, I was a whole mountain away, thinking I was heading back to camp, totally turned around. Somehow within ten minutes of that prayer, they found me and got me back to the camp. When I woke up the next morning, I saw a foot of snow on the ground. I surely would have died if God had not saved me.

One of my favorite Scriptures is Isaiah 50:4, *"The Lord God has given me the tongue of the learned, that I would have a word in season for him who is weary. . . He awakens my ear, morning by morning."* Once my family was visiting my parents in Charlotte, North Carolina, because I had a little time off from traveling. As many people know, I am not an early morning person, so when I heard my name, "Ryan, Ryan, Ryan," I popped one eye open and saw that the sun was not even up and I got irritated. I could not tell if it was a man's voice or a woman's voice, but I did not hear any of my little children crying for me to come, so I did not understand what could be going on. I was so tired. I turned over in Kelly's direction and said, "What?"—And she was still sound asleep. So I thought, "Oh man, I must be dreaming or something," and I went back to sleep.

I heard it again, "Ryan, Ryan...," and this time I could tell that it was God. Every hair on my body stood on end. I sat up again. I couldn't believe my wife was not hearing this—or everyone else in the house, for that matter. Then the voice said to me, "Didn't you ask me to awaken your ear morning by morning?" Never in my wildest dreams did I think God was going to audibly wake me up because of a Scripture I had quoted. Along with it came such a strong pull to come and be with Him. Sometimes, we don't have these kinds of encounters because we are not really believing that they are available for us.

Out of Body Experiences

Other terms for an out of body experience are being "translated" or "transported." This means your spirit is literally taken out of your body and transported to another location for a while, or your whole body is transported instantly into another geographical place. I personally use the term "transported" for when someone is taken spirit, soul, and body, and transported by God to another location. God transported Philip in Acts 8:39-40. Philip was in one location, the Spirit carried him away, and Philip found himself in another location. I personally use the word "translated" for when someone is taken "in the spirit" to another location. In other words, their body stays in one place but they travel to another location in the spirit. Ezekiel was taken out of his body and taken to Jerusalem, which he saw in the form of visions (see Ezek. 8).

People should not let the enemy's version of this experience make the real thing worrisome. This is not the same as astral projection or whatever term New Agers prefer, which is the demonic counterfeit of God's spirit travel.

Traveling in the realm of the spirit is not something that you can seek after. You do not ask God to take you out of your body, nor do you attempt it on your own. Traveling in the realm of the spirit is a byproduct of being in a relationship with God.

The first time it happened to me, I was lying in my bed in Tennessee. The next morning, I was scheduled to get on an airplane bound for a ministry trip to London, England. I had never been there before. I had just asked the Lord what He might want me to say to this pastor and his church, when suddenly I went into a vision. In the vision, I saw myself hovering over and moving through a city. Again, I had never traveled there before, so I thought it must be prophetically symbolic. I saw certain buildings with certain words on the signs. I saw certain architecture with a certain color of exterior paint. I saw statues. And the Lord told me to prophesy over the leader of the church, and to mention the year that something had happened in their building, which He showed me.

The next day, I got on the plane and flew to London. There, I saw everything I had seen in the spirit the night before. I saw the buildings with certain words on the signs, I saw statues. I saw the same paint colors and everything. Only then did I realize that I actually had traveled there the previous night. The Holy Spirit had translated me. I would have thought that it would be an incredible experience, but I experienced it in a really natural way. It happened just as I was enjoying fellowship with God!

Why Is Experiencing the Glory of God Important?

The Glory of God changes a person. In fact, it requires God and His Glory in order to change and transform a person. Second Corinthians 3:18 says that only as we behold the glory of God with an unveiled face are we transformed into the same image, from one degree of glory to another. What you behold, you become. We were created to behold God, to become like Him, and to display His goodness to all who come in contact with us.

We need the presence of God in our lives, and we need to welcome Him in whatever way He wants to come to us. So, whether He comes to you in visions, dreams, trances, audible voices, angelic visitations, open heavens, out-of-body experiences, a still small voice or whisper in your spirit, or anything else from His "menu," you need to make a commitment to the Lord that you will guard and nurture what He deposits into your life, and truly live a supernatural lifestyle!

Chapter 9

Established in the Supernatural

It should seem obvious to us that our God is a supernatural God and we are His people, so therefore we are also supernatural. Well, that sounds good in theory, and most believers would agree to this "in theory." However, when one begins to actually truly experience the supernatural side of our God, it becomes something that our natural mind cannot accept (see 1 Cor. 2:14); therefore, in the church today there is a great battle over the supernatural.

Now, I readily admit that all sorts of fruity, flakey, nutty nonsense is going on in the church, all "in the name of Jesus" and in "being supernatural." I also readily admit that satan is a great deceiver and will do everything he can to deceive Christians into dabbling into all kinds of New-Age or occult activity and therefore we should be very careful in this area.

It is for those reasons that I have written this book. My goal in this book has been for you, the reader, to come to a personal understanding from the Bible that God is supernatural, the church is supernatural, you are supernatural, and you are called to live a supernatural lifestyle.

The Christian life is supposed to be one that is balanced between Word and Spirit. However, I see many believers today who are afraid of anything "in the Spirit." This should not be. Many have more faith in the devil to deceive them than they do in God to protect them and lead them into their inheritance of a supernatural lifestyle. The Bible says in Matthew 7:7-11 (ESV):

> *Ask, and it will be given to you; seek, and you will find; knock, and it will be opened to you. For everyone who asks receives, and the one who seeks finds, and to the one who knocks it will be opened. Or which one of you, if his son asks him for bread, will give him a stone? Or if he asks for a fish, will give him a serpent? If you then, who are evil, know how to give good gifts to your children, how much more will your Father who is in heaven give good things to those who ask him!*

We need to put our trust and faith in God as our Father, having the boldness to *ask* Him for the reality of the supernatural in our lives. This boldness to believe that living in the supernatural is your legal right according to Scripture can only come as you get a revelation of your identity, according to Scripture. The son of a king would never doubt that it is his right to enjoy his father's kingdom, because he knows that he is the son of the king!

Your Supernatural Identity

Let's quickly review a few powerful truths...

As a believer in Jesus Christ, you did not just join some religious social club when you got saved and became a Christian. You were literally "born again" or "born from above" (see John 3:3). In your natural birth you were "born of your parents," but in your spiritual birth (your born-again experience with Christ) you were "born of God" (see John 1:12-13). Apples bring forth apples, oranges bring forth oranges, your parents brought you forth at your birth, and at your new-birth, God "brought you forth." Don't you get it? You can't help being like your parents in some ways...you were born of them! In the same way, you can't help being supernatural...you have been born of God!

In that born-again experience you became a new creature, a new creation (see 2 Cor. 5:17). The Holy Spirit came into and mingled with your human spirit and you are now "one spirit" with Him (see 1 Cor. 6:17). In your natural birth you were born into the line or lineage of the first Adam, and therefore under the curse. In your new birth you were born of and into the line or lineage of the *last* Adam, Jesus Christ. You were freed from the curse, but you were also brought into a brand new supernatural life and plane of existence. Check out this amazing Scripture passage in First Corinthians 15:45-49 (ESV):

> *Thus it is written, "The first man Adam became a living being"; the last Adam became a life-giving spirit. But it is not the spiritual that is first but the natural, and then the spiritual. The first man was from the earth, a man of dust; the second man is from heaven. As was the man of dust, so also are those who are of the dust, and*

as is the man of heaven, so also are those who are
of heaven. Just as we have borne the image of the
man of dust, we shall also bear the image of the
man of heaven.

Isn't that incredible! You were once of Adam, but now as is the man of Heaven, the Last Adam—Jesus Christ, so also are those who are of Him...they are of Heaven. It's as if your spiritual umbilical cord has been unplugged from the natural man, Adam, and plugged into the supernatural, heavenly man, the Last Adam—Christ Jesus! You are supernatural and were created to live supernaturally. You are now seated with Christ in heavenly places (see Eph. 2:6).

A Citizen of the Kingdom of Heaven

You are now a citizen of the Kingdom of Heaven. Not after you die and go to Heaven. No, you are *now* a citizen of the Kingdom of Heaven (see Phil. 3:20). Your primary citizenship is no longer of your nation or even of the earth. Of course, you are still a citizen of your nation, but your "primary" citizenship is now of Heaven. Yes, one day Jesus will transform your lowly earthly body into a fully glorified body and you will experience dimensions of Heaven that you are not currently able to experience in this human body. However, right *now* you are a citizen of Heaven and have been born of God, and through your "spiritual senses" you can ask God that it would be *"on earth as it is in Heaven"* in your life (see Matt. 6:10).

God's Kingdom has a culture, and it is a supernatural culture. What exactly is the meaning of "culture," you might ask? Culture is defined as *a set of shared values, atti-tudes, behaviors, goals, and practices that characterize a society.* Basically, culture is your way of life. It also includes the art and music of a culture. God's Kingdom has a culture. As a citizen of the Kingdom of Heaven, His supernatural culture is now to be your culture. In a sense, this book has been one long introduction to the culture, or way of life, in God's supernatural Kingdom culture. We have talked about the specific language of His culture and how God communicates to us, and we also talked about the various kinds of experiences you will have in God's supernatural realm.

This supernatural lifestyle was natural for the believers in the Book of Acts. They allowed their entire lives to be directed in supernatural ways. For example:

Ananias delivered a message from God to Saul of Tarsus (the murderer of Christians) because God spoke to him in a vision. Saul became Paul the Apostle (see Acts 9:10-19).

Peter took the Gospel to the gentiles for the first time because he had a vision in a trance while sitting on his rooftop, of a white sheet coming down from Heaven with four-footed animals on it. This was his explanation that he gave to the other leaders, and they bought into it and recognized it as God speaking because they understood and lived by the supernatural language and culture of God's Kingdom (see Acts 10:9 to 11:18).

The disciples were praying for Peter to be released from prison. God sent an angel to release Peter. Peter knocked on the door where the disciples were meeting. Rhoda freaked out and told them Peter was at the door.

The disciples instead believed that there was an angel (materialized in the flesh) standing at the door instead of Peter. (Don't tell me angelic visitations are not for today. They were obviously so common in the Book of Acts that the disciples had more faith to believe that an angel was standing at the door than to actually believe that God had answered their prayer and that Peter was actually standing at their door!) (See Acts 12:6-17.)

These are just a few among dozens of supernatural moments in the lives of the early disciples. The Book of Acts church was the baby church. Not only should we be experiencing the same supernatural lifestyle today, but it is going to increase in the earth the closer we get to the return of Jesus.

A Great Awakening

I have often likened the church to a terrorist sleeper cell. Now before you laugh at me, just let me explain. With a terrorist sleeper cell, a person is sent into another nation and told to blend in and live a normal life. They often go to college, get married, and maybe even have children. But then one day they get a phone call and their purpose in life is activated and they begin to fulfill their purpose of being a terrorist. The Church is like a sleeping giant. A sleeping giant that has forgotten her purpose.

There is a great awakening that I believe is sweeping the earth right now. The Holy Spirit is waking up the church, the Bride of Christ. In this awakening, the church is finding a passion for Jesus again. We are being wooed and fascinated by the message of divine love and intimacy with our Bridegroom King, Jesus. From this place of passion, the church is being awakened to purpose. Our purpose is to be the very gateway of Heaven on the earth. Our purpose is to be the corporate Body of Christ and to demonstrate the goodness, love, and power of God's Kingdom to the world around us, just as Jesus did when He walked the earth.

In this awakening, the church is being drawn out from the world system and the world cultures and is being taught a new way to live...a supernatural way to live. This was modeled for us by the nation of Israel. They were delivered from the bondage of a dark kingdom just as we have been delivered from the kingdom of darkness. Israel then found themselves in the middle of a wilderness, having not yet stepped into what God had destined for them to step into, in their lifetime. Likewise, the church is at an "in-between" place where we've been saved and redeemed but have not yet stepped into our inheritance that God has destined for the church to walk in, on this side of eternity.

You see, in the wilderness, Israel was taught a new way to live. Moses was taken up the mountain and into the glory of God, and in that supernatural glory, God delivered a brand new supernatural culture to Israel. Moses came down from the mountain and delivered this new culture that included a tabernacle, a priest-hood, a system of sacrifices and feasts, and so on. If Israel would begin to live by this new culture, then God and His glory would abide in their midst as a nation. When the people lived the way they were instructed, then Israel was powerful and began to advance toward their Promised Land of destiny.

A Supernatural Kingdom Culture

Today, God is challenging His Bride, His Church, to rise up out of the cultures of this world and even out of what we've learned of dry, stale, religious culture. What are we being called to rise into? Into the supernatural culture of the Kingdom of God, just like the church was birthed into in the Book of Acts. This current awakening is also manifesting as a great shaking. God is shaking His Church. He is shaking everything that is not of Him. He is shaking every world system that we have put our trust in. He is shaking all our man-made ideas of who He is and how He does things. He is shaking everything that can be shaken. He is shaking our entire world and religious culture. What is His goal in all this shaking? He wants His Bride to find herself standing upon only one thing...the Rock—Jesus Christ. He wants to establish us in the supernatural lifestyle of liberty and freedom that we were created for. He wants to empower us for advancement. But make no mistake about it. We all, like Israel in the wilderness, are on a journey, a journey that is meant to lead us to Him and into this incredible realm of supernatural living!

The Journey—Nothing but Dependence Upon Him

This whole book has been my attempt to help get you started on this journey of supernatural living. The learning and discovery process goes on for your entire lifetime. God is absolutely amazing, and you can search Him out and discover more about Him and experience more of Him for an entire lifetime, but you will just simply discover that He is endless. God is so vast that we will spend a lifetime discovering more of Him and worshiping Him for Who He is!

I have people come up to me all the time to say, "Ryan, I went through your School of the Supernatural and I did everything that you said to do. But I still do not have what you have."

I always answer, "Wow, how long did you practice these things you learned in the School?

"Oh man, a whole week, a whole month. I just soaked for like eight hours a day for a whole month."

I reply, "Wow, I applaud you. It took over fifteen years of my life to begin to actually 'live' this supernatural lifestyle that I am living today, and I feel like I am only beginning to live in the fullness of God's revelation."

How exciting it is to receive this awesome revelation of what God has made available for us, and oh, how exciting it is to taste of it and actually live in the fullness of our destiny. Those are the two moments that excite us. Yet, the moments that are the most exciting for God are the in-between ones. God's favorite part is the journey itself, because He gets to relate to us, teach us, guide us, and love us. We may not enjoy all of it, but He does.

The supernatural life is impossible for someone to do in the natural. Any calling from God that you may have is impossible for you to do on your own. But your God will bring you to a place in your journey where you know nothing else but dependence upon Him. Supernatural living requires dependence upon Him, and dependence requires brokenness, humility, patience, and commitment.

Living in the supernatural—I am not talking about having a supernatural encounter, I am talking about *living* in the supernatural—will require your life. It is the basic Gospel message: *"I have been crucified with Christ; and it is no longer I who live, but Christ lives in me; and the life which I now live in the flesh I live by faith in the Son of God, who loved me and gave Himself up for me"* (Gal. 2:20 NASB).

Jesus wants to excite you and thrill you and show you the things of the Kingdom. Then He wants to start working on you to transform you into the kind of person you need to be to carry the fullness of Him that He has destined for you to share with the world around you.

> *Such is the confidence that we have through Christ towards God. Not that we are sufficient in ourselves to claim anything as coming from us, but our sufficiency is from God, who has made us competent to be ministers of a new covenant, not of the letter but of the Spirit. For the letter kills, but the Spirit gives life* (2 Corinthians 3:4 ESV).

You will not make much progress if you just put this book down and go back to your normal lifestyle. You need to take the initiative to step into intimacy with Jesus Christ and thereby into a supernatural lifestyle, and you need to keep doing it, consistently and deliberately and faithfully. *He* is worth the sacrifice and hard work. Living in God's heavenly realm is like a supernatural feast—and you do not have to wait for Heaven to enjoy it.

However, as I mentioned in the first chapter of this book, it requires a genuine lifestyle of being a consecrated priest. It requires that daily maintenance of learning to give yourself to God. It requires you living a life before an audience of One and spending yourself on Him, because He is worthy! It requires that lifestyle of worship and intimacy at His feet.

If you take one thing away from this book, let it be this: you were created for intimacy with Him! Living a supernatural lifestyle is simply a byproduct of enjoying God. Nothing in this life compares to the surpassing worth of knowing Jesus Christ!

Prayer of Impartation

I want to pray for you as you begin the most amazing journey of your life. The journey of supernatural discovery of our great God!

> *Father, for those reading this book right now at this moment, I pray that You would empower them, by Your love, to be catapulted into this amazingly supernatural lifestyle that You created them for. Carry them away into that intoxicatingly wonderful place of Your love and glory presence. Begin to saturate them with Your goodness. Like Elisha prayed for his servant, Lord, I pray that You would open their eyes that they may see. As they present their spiritual senses to You, open them up and sensitize them to the wonders of Your supernatural kingdom! I ask this in Jesus' name! Amen!*

RYAN
WYATT

ABIDING GLORY
CHURCH & INTERNATIONAL MINISTRY BASE

Ryan Wyatt is the host of the TV show "Abiding Glory with Ryan Wyatt", as well as the Founder and Senior Leader of Abiding Glory Church & International Ministry Base, located in Knoxville, TN, which includes:

* Abiding Glory Church
* Abiding Glory TV
* Abiding Glory Kingdom Network (an apostolic network of ministries, and churches)
* Abiding Glory Kingdom Institute (Bible college)
* Cry For Justice (pulling women and children out of modern-day sex slavery)
* The Life Restoration Center (wholeness center for spirit, soul and body)
* and more to come...

Ryan has an apostolic calling to raise up an army of believers to establish and expand the Kingdom of God, "on Earth as it is in Heaven". His church and ministry is marked by a strong miracle-healing anointing as well as a unique and inspiring prophetic teaching gift that launches believers into new dimensions of intimacy, power and supernatural lifestyle with God while also establishing a healthy balance and foundation in the Word of God, with Godly Character.

Ryan believes that the same presence, power, love and character that Jesus manifested in His single human body He will also manifest through His corporate body, the church. There is a church that Jesus is building and that He burns with passion for. Ryan has a heart to see the church become all she is destined to be! To this end, Ryan focuses on training both ministry leaders and believers so they can be equipped for the work of ministry, and released as a mighty army, establishing and expanding the Kingdom of God in every sphere of culture, all throughout the Earth.

Ryan, his wife Kelly, and their three sons live in Knoxville, TN.

MORE RESOURCES BY THE AUTHOR

SCHOOL OF THE SUPERNATURAL: BECOMING A HABITATION OF GOD

Get the DVD or CD set of the School of the Supernatural along with a set of manuals for your church or small group and open them up to Authentic Biblical Christianity. Teach them to activate their spiritual senses and engage a life of supernatural encounter with God in the Heavenly Realm.

HOSTING THE HOLY SPIRIT

How do we build a landing strip and orchestrate our lives so that we become a resting place for the Holy Spirit? By creating an atmosphere where the Holy Spirit is comfortable and longing to reside, we can become a living habitation of God's tangible glory. There are key milestones within this process as God literally transforms you into a living, breathing revival that infiltrates every part of society in everyday life. This powerful teaching will help unlock your understanding and launch you headlong into one of the most precious and important journeys of your life!

THE OVERSHADOWING

The Overshadowing is a spontaneous non-stop journey into the presence of God! This CD was not designed to be a typical CD for your musical enjoyment, but rather an experience that will lead you into an encounter with the Glory of God.

MANY OTHER ANOINTED RESOURCES AVAILABLE
VISIT ABIDINGGLORY.COM OR
CALL **865-573-8008** TODAY!

In the right hands, This Book will Change Lives!

Most of the people who need this message will not be looking for this book. To change their lives, you need to put a copy of this book in their hands.

> *But others (seeds) fell into good ground, and brought forth fruit, some a hundred-fold, some sixty-fold, some thirty-fold* (Matthew 13:8).

Our ministry is constantly seeking methods to find the good ground, the people who need this anointed message to change their lives. Will you help us reach these people?

> *Remember this—a farmer who plants only a few seeds will get a small crop. But the one who plants generously will get a generous crop* (2 Corinthians 9:6).

EXTEND THIS MINISTRY BY SOWING
3 BOOKS, 5 BOOKS, 10 BOOKS, OR MORE TODAY,
AND BECOME A LIFE CHANGER!

Thank you,

Don Nori Sr., Publisher
Destiny Image
Since 1982

DESTINY IMAGE PUBLISHERS, INC.

*"Speaking to the Purposes of God for This Generation
and for the Generations to Come."*

VISIT OUR NEW SITE HOME AT
WWW.DESTINYIMAGE.COM

FREE SUBSCRIPTION TO DI NEWSLETTER

Receive free unpublished articles by top DI authors, exclusive

discounts, and free downloads from our best and newest books.

Visit www.destinyimage.com to subscribe.

Write to: Destiny Image
                P.O. Box 310
                Shippensburg, PA 17257-0310

    Call: 1-800-722-6774

    Email: orders@destinyimage.com

For a complete list of our titles or to place an order
online, visit www.destinyimage.com.